Business Practices, Biblical Promises

Larry Scanlan

Printed by Kindle Direct Publishing

© 2018 **Larry Scanlan**

All rights reserved.

Manufactured in the United States of America

ISBN-13: 9781731412744

NOTE: The information in this book is true and complete to the best of the author's knowledge. The author and the publisher disclaim all liability in connection with the use of this book.

All scripture quotations, unless otherwise indicated, are taken from the Holy Bible, New International Version, NIV, Life Application Study Bible. Copyrighted 1973, 1978, 1984, 2011 by Biblica, Inc. Published jointly by Tyndale House Publishers, Inc. and Zondervan. All rights reserved worldwide. www.zondervan.com. "New International Version" and "NIV" are trademarks registered in the United States Patent and Trademark office by Biblica, Inc.

All rights reserved. No portion of this book may be reproduced or transmitted in any form whatsoever by any means—electronic, mechanical, photocopy, recording, scanning or other—without the prior written permission of the author and publisher except for brief quotations in critical reviews or articles.

Business Practices, Biblical Promises

*How to Use Biblical Principles
to Make Better Business Decisions*

Larry Scanlan

Larry Scanlan

Praise for Larry Scanlan's Work...

"Finally, a Christian book for business leaders written by an author with a deep personal faith and spiritual commitment. As a business associate and friend for many years, I have seen first-hand how Larry applies God's Word to our work...and reaps the rewards. The Bible says 'faith without works is dead.' Here's a down-to-earth primer that all business people can use to live out their faith through their everyday work life."
  – Philip Beauchamp, LFACHE, President and CEO, (retired)
    Morton Plant Mease Healthcare, Inc.

"I have known Larry Scanlan for more than a decade and benefit significantly in business and life from his sage advice and outstanding example. He is an unwavering 'good and faithful servant' leader with a powerful purpose to make people better decision makers while keeping true to their faith. The readers of this book will now have the great fortune his colleagues and friends have had for many years as they learn directly from Larry's personal experiences and reflections. They will find his approach masterful and his wisdom unmatched."
  – James Mergiotti
    Retired President of Peirce College

"Larry has served as my professional mentor for many years. Any time I have a question on the direction I should be taking, I reach out to him for guidance. Larry is purposeful and thoughtful in his advice, always guiding me to consider the impact of decisions on personal and professional situations. His wisdom and grace are evident through not only his words, but through his actions. Larry's personal experience and practical advice in this gem of a book—and the reflection and action steps in each chapter—will help countless readers truly fulfill their God-given purpose, make better business decisions and ultimately live better, more balanced lives."
  – Barbara Bryan, Healthcare Consulting Executive and
    Former Founding Partner of Invalesco Group, Inc.

Larry Scanlan

DEDICATION

First to my wife Connie for her love and for her God-given gift of encouragement making a difference in my life as well as those of her family, friends and former co-workers;

To healthcare professionals and educators who have the opportunity every day to make a God-given difference in the lives of others;

To first responders, like my grandparents, great-grandparents, a special uncle, and other relatives who risk their lives so others may live;

In memory of Becky Rust, my long-time, excellent administrative assistant who passed away in 2017 while in the middle of helping me with this project;

To each of you who desire to make decisions to impart a God honoring difference in the life of your family, business, church and community. God will honor the desires of your heart!

Larry Scanlan

Business Practices, Biblical Promises

TABLE OF CONTENTS

Introduction..xi

Part I: It's About Degrees and Titles...*Or Is It?*

Chapter 1: Are You Willing to Make a Difference? 3

Chapter 2: Talent, Teamwork and Training...21

Chapter 3: Making Wise Decisions: Heart Matters................................45

Chapter 4: Making Wise Decisions: Head Matters................................63

Part II: Our Plan Will Carry the Day...*Or Will It?*

Chapter 5: Vision and Mission: *Where* Are We Going and *Why*.................91

Chapter 6: Planning: *How* Will We Accomplish Our Goals? 109

Chapter 7: Priorities: Are We *Doing* What We Planned? 129

Chapter 8: Metrics and Milestones: *Measuring* Our Progress................151

Part III: When Things Go South It Means I Failed... *Or Does It?*

Chapter 9: Testing and Trials: Stuff Happens…Or It Soon Will! 177

Chapter 10: Complacency and Compromise: Twin Killers of Businesses and Careers..197

Chapter 11: Profiles in Perseverance...221

Chapter 12: Legacies and Epitaphs: Finishing Strong.......................241

Acknowledgments..265

Larry Scanlan

INTRODUCTION

The business decisions we make reveal our spiritual orientation and ultimately define our effectiveness within a profession. How do we live out our faith and make a difference in the place where we spend the most significant portion of our waking day, the business world, while it distances itself from Judeo-Christian tenets?

Most of us not only spend significant time at work, we take it home and even on vacation with us. Is it all about making a paycheck, meeting our company's numbers, advancing our career, and adhering to the latest edict of political correctness? Where does our family fit in? Can we love bosses, colleagues, team members and customers, many of whom may not share our values? How do we make sound faith-based decisions in this competitive and complex business world?

During my career, going on fifty years at the time of this writing, I have been chief financial officer of two organizations. In addition I have been president of two hospitals and the president or managing director of three national healthcare consulting firms. I have led both for-profit and non-profit companies. I currently serve on two boards, one a healthcare system, the other a private college. I am also a Certified Public Accountant and a Fellow of the Healthcare Financial Management Association. Over the years I have also had the responsibility of serving as a trustee and as a deacon in several churches.

I mention this background because I know first-hand it's not easy to run a business. Nor is it easy to work for a company. In fact both are getting harder. It's challenging to find the ideal job, and keeping it is no guarantee. Working in an occupation or profession and making a difference that matters is challenging.

Thankfully the power of the gospel makes faith, love, action and change possible even in the business world. The Bible is not silent on the kind of times in which we find ourselves. Nor is it silent on the place of business in society and the responsibilities of its leaders and followers. In fact the Bible's relevancy is surreal. Most of Jesus' interactions while on this earth were in the marketplace.

Decisions we make about work define the priority God and family have in our lives. Business decisions dictate what we deem important in all phases of life, thus having profound consequences at work, home and in our neighborhoods. Our decisions reveal the reality of the faith we profess while defining the integrity of our personhood.

What can you and I do? This book is an encouraging call to make decisions which impact matters beyond meeting our company's numbers and the urgency of conformity. It is comprised of three practical parts which combine contemporary work place scenarios with Biblical business stories. These will guide the reader on how to make a difference that goes beyond quarterly targets and cultural trends. We as a faith-based people can either go along with the crowd, or we can act on the faith we profess.

Part I will challenge the reader's willingness to make a difference through wise decision making. You don't need a fancy title to make a difference; however, knowing when to step-up, step-back, or step-out determines the effectiveness of our impact. We'll examine how to make wise decisions, exploring the motives of our heart and the soundness of our thinking. *How* we make decisions determines the long-term success or failure of our business unit, career, and life. Enough said.

Part II tests our planning skills within our own sphere of influence. Each of us has an area of influence in our work. These four chapters speak to our vision, mission, and priorities as we address the key components of practical planning. In addition we'll discuss the metrics used for judging business and career success in the context of God's standards. The Bible has plenty to say about how we measure performance and determine success.

Part III we'll address what happens far too often—things don't go as planned. We have all been in this situation. When things go south does it mean we failed? How do we respond and take the long view? The reader will be encouraged that our careers and legacies are not determined by our bosses or the circumstances of an adverse situation. You can make a difference no matter how challenging your current or past situations have been.

Each chapter of the book will conclude with a self-assessment comprised of a few simple reflection questions, followed by practical action steps for the reader's consideration and follow-up.

One person can make a difference. Two or more can be particularly powerful. Our businesses and communities need difference makers, men and women with wisdom who are grounded, tested, and trusted. We each have a choice. We can silently and sullenly go along with the culture or we can be disciples, acting out of love in our homes and in our business world. You can make decisions that really matter! What follows will help you make a difference.

Part I:

It's About Degrees and Titles... *Or Is It?*

Larry Scanlan

Chapter 1

Are You Willing to Make a Difference?

Michele picked up a call in her office at 8:15 a.m. Thursday from her boss, Edward. He said he'd received a request for a proposal for a potentially substantial project and it had an extremely tight turnaround. It had to be electronically transmitted to the prospective client no later than noon Saturday, a little more than forty-eight hours away.

She had a fancy title for a position which, in reality, was an administrative assistant. In a company that offered consulting services to a half-dozen industries, Edward headed up one of the firm's divisions that constituted the largest slice of the company's revenue pie.

Edward asked Michele, given the tight deadline and complexity of the project, if she thought she could pull the proposal together in time for his review. She responded that she was excited about heading it, fully realizing she would have to cajole at least a dozen or more people to provide input into their respective pieces of the proposal. This would be no easy matter, especially with many consultants either out of town or traveling to or from their various assignments. It was indeed a significant project, one that would generate fees of over three million dollars and keep twenty-eight consultants busy for the next three to four months.

The call from Edward ended with words that would resonate with Michele: "Remember, this proposal can't go out without my blessing." Michele jumped right into tackling the proposal, calling almost two dozen other professionals to seek their input that day. She received a high level of cooperation, as everyone understood the significance of the potential project. Many of the consultants felt the firm's skill sets gave them an inside edge toward winning the bid. She worked until ten p.m. Thursday, leaving the office with a feeling of "I got this."

Michele spent Friday morning reviewing, editing and proofing the firm's response. She made sure every question was fully answered and the accuracy of the information was credible. This included the rationale for the proposed pricing which Edward would especially need to focus upon and approve. It had been an exhausting day-and-a-half, but the satisfaction of knowing the firm would have a solid chance to win this potential client provided her with a rush of adrenalin to get it done.

All she needed now was for her boss to review and sign off on the firm's proposal. Michele e-mailed it to Edward early Friday afternoon. Receiving no response, she texted him about ninety minutes later. Still she received no reply. Becoming anxious, she called him, but the call went straight to voice mail. She remembered his words: "This can't go out without my blessing." She frantically sent several more e-mails and texts and made several more calls. And still she got no reply. She left work in a state of anxiety late Friday evening and only got a few hours of sleep that night.

Michele cancelled her Saturday morning plans and instead went into the office. Several more rounds of e-mails, texts and phone calls to Edward were met with silence. By 11 a.m. she was in full panic mode, and at 11:30 a.m. she broke down at her desk and cried. She stared at her computer and phone as the clock struck noon, stunned at what had just happened. The firm had lost its chance, given the prospective client's board of directors was meeting at that very hour to review the submitted proposals and make its selection. She sat numbly in shock in front of her computer until 12:45 p.m. then called her friend to cancel plans they had made for the afternoon. Once home, she grabbed a bottle of wine and retreated to her bedroom for the rest of the day.

On Monday morning Michele was eager to confront her boss about his lack of availability and responsiveness. When Edward finally returned her call on Monday afternoon he calmly explained that he had gone to his vacation home for the weekend and decided not to take messages. He then changed the subject without any apology or recognition of her herculean effort to pull the proposal together. She felt dismissed, defeated, devastated…as if she did not matter.

Larry Scanlan

Leadership vacuums: unintended consequences

This was not the first time a partner in this firm missed a proposal deadline and thus forfeited the company's opportunity to win work, but for Michele it was the last straw. Within four weeks she found another job and several years later she formed her own marketing firm. Ironically, she now helps companies win more business. As for the consulting firm, it missed its revenue and profitability targets that quarter and laid off dozens of consultants; however, Edward was not one of them.

This story is real, only the names are changed to protect the real leader from the paid leader!

When there are leadership vacuums such as described above, the Bible predicts what will happen in such circumstances. In the Old Testament Book of Judges, between chapters seventeen and twenty-one, we read this quote no less than four times: "In those days Israel had no king." Substitute the word *leader* for king and *company* for Israel, and this is the situation we are talking about here now. Judges concludes with this: "In those days Israel had no king, everyone did as he saw fit." (Judges 21:25)

Edward could do what he wanted because those above him placed little accountability on him for being sure proposals were completed and delivered on time. The book of Judges describes leaders like Edward who took advantage of people who were lower in title and position, doing what they pleased whenever it suited them. For instance, a tribe known as the Danites sought territory and property by seeking to take advantage of people unlikely to resist their self-centered agenda. (Judges 18)

Culture can compromise us…or embolden us.

Leaders set the tone at the top. Culture speaks to the way a company does business, how things are done. Decision makers determine what is important and what is not, which contributes to defining a company's culture. A culture created by dishonest or unethical leaders often has adverse emotional and financial consequences on those under their watch, and a leadership vacuum can cause confusion, conflict and even chaos.

Michele had time stolen she could not get back, working evenings and on Saturday. In addition, mental fatigue exhausted her as she worried whether there would be sufficient work in her company's pipeline for her to remain employed.

It is often difficult for workers in compromised cultures to go against the tide of an organization's hierarchy and unwritten morass of political correctness. But sometimes they find opportunities to do something positive and constructive as a result.

Michele did not believe she could take the bold step of reporting the incident involving Edward. Instead, she chose to leave the company. Such is often the outcome in companies where there are poor leaders or a leadership vacuum.

Larry Scanlan

Should you step up? Step back? Or step out?

Leadership requires a willingness to make decisions that make a difference. You don't need a title to be a leader.

Many know the Bible story of David and Goliath. We sometimes forget some of the important details leading up to this epic one-on-one battle. The Philistines and the Israelites had lined up on opposite sides of a valley day after day, glaring and shouting at each other without making a move. Given the steep ravine, neither side wanted to be the first to launch out because they likely would incur heavy casualties. Though success was desired they did not want to take the risk.

It's like that in business as well. I have worked with companies that had a chance to pull ahead of their competitors by executing a breakaway strategy; however, achieving that reward meant taking considerable risks the companies' leaders were unwilling to take.

Leaders are responsible for evaluating risk-reward scenarios. There are usually three predominant options:

- Go for it: some decision makers discern advancing a cause or a mission is indeed worthy of its inherent risk. They go for the prize, they're "all in."
- Status quo: management may choose to make a "career" decision to stick with the current state, being careful not to jeopardize their positions, titles and compensation packages.

- Wait and see: finally, some leaders or aspiring leaders will judge the timing of the business risk not to be right—waiting for another competitor to go first and perhaps fail, thereby learning from their opponent's mistakes. Why wait? Because so-called leading-edge companies sometimes become "bleeding edge" enterprises when they misjudge risk.

This third scenario was taking place in the story of David and Goliath on the rims of the Valley of Elah between two military competitors, each desiring to win but waiting for the other to make the first move. Each day Goliath, over nine feet tall, would challenge his opponents to a one-on-one survivor fight, winner take all. The Israelites were scared and demoralized, given the seeming invincibility of this oversized competitor.

As forty days passed by, young David was asked by his father to go check on the status of the battle. David's brothers were not thrilled to see him; they thought he just came to watch, not initially realizing he was sent to bring them food.

When David observed the situation and asked questions he thought he could make a difference in this particular situation, having a breakaway strategy in mind. He offered to fight the far bigger and more experienced warrior whom all other men feared. He was willing to take a risk to step up and change the stalemate.

David made his case to King Saul. Although he was young, he

had what we call "street creds" (smarts). His strategy was based on his experience of taking down bears and lions; he felt prepared to make a difference. Every other person on the battlefield saw the path to success involved substantial career risk. David, however, saw an opportunity to execute a successful strategy.

Saul decided to bet the company on David and his idea. Shortly thereafter David filled the leadership vacuum, took down the giant with his slingshot and won the battle. (1 Samuel 17: 1-50) His career took off with this one memorable and courageous act of stepping into a challenge in need of direct and creative leadership.

In one of my early consulting assignments I worked with a healthcare organization that owned two hospitals. One, the flagship entity, had been in operation for many years. It was located in a stable but older area of the county with no realistic growth prospects. Years before, a former CEO of this organization had the foresight to buy a parcel of land in another part of the same county. The board of trustees reluctantly went along and approved the purchase, even though most thought the land was "out in the sticks," thinking the transaction was more foolish than visionary.

A few years later the board approved constructing their second hospital on this land but with only limited services since it did not have enough money to build a full-service hospital. The trustees were so embarrassed by this "half-hospital" they refused to even hold their meetings in it. The new hospital was struggling. It did not even have dedicated management, as executives of the flagship enterprise were to oversee the newer entity but were rarely on site.

When our consulting firm was contracted to help them it became clear this location was in a growth corridor and would go a long way to ensuring the future viability of the organization.

As we immersed ourselves into the engagement, observed operations and interviewed people, it became obvious that a woman we'll call Robin got things done. She was not the president, or even a vice-president, she was a nurse with expertise in emergency management; however, she understood that the hospital staff needed direction in carrying out their patient care responsibilities. Robin would schedule and adjust staffing to meet the ebbs and flows of patient volumes, order supplies, and generally keep day to day operations running. Employees knew they could turn to her to get decisions made and get things done. She filled the leadership vacuum.

The apostle Peter wrote to his followers that they, as leaders, were to shepherd those under their watch, "not because you must, but because you are willing, as God wants you to be." (1 Peter 5:2) Robin was that kind of professional. Management at the flagship hospital likely did not appreciate the role or the magnitude of the contribution she played in bringing this new hospital to life. But that didn't matter to Robin. She provided decisive leadership in the absence of a full-time, on-site administrator because it was needed.

Fortunately, our consulting team convinced the board and management to dedicate executive talent to overseeing further development of the new campus. We then guided them through a merger so that they could access the capital required to expand the entity into a full-service hospital. Once achieved this former "half-hospital" went on to be one of the top performing hospitals in a well-respected ten hospital system. Moreover, it has been named numerous times as one of the top community hospitals nationwide.

Robin eventually went on to another challenge at a bigger organization. Having accomplished her goals at the hospital, she went into consulting. Now, over twelve years later, she still works for the same company, mentoring others and making a difference for her company's clients nationwide.

Making a difference for others

Leadership begins when we willingly accept the opportunity to make a difference to help people…like King David did, like Robin did. Most of us have such opportunities if we are alert to them.

Jesus himself often set the example of both being aware of and meeting people's needs; he did more than preach His Gospel message. In one occasion Jesus was concerned about sending a large group of people home on a long journey without first feeding them so that they would have strength and energy for their travels. It was no small gathering but a massive horde of about four-thousand people. The disciples' reaction to Jesus' desire to meet this very basic need was interesting, as they fretted about how to feed such a large crowd (perhaps they had an "ain't our job" mentality). Jesus, of course, met the need in a miraculous way and, like we usually experience in our own social gatherings, there was plenty of food left over. (Mark 8:1-9)

Lest you think Jesus "played" to very large crowds, later in this same chapter (and in many other chapters in the Gospels) an individual had a need, this time a blind man. Discerning his need, Jesus took the time to heal him. Whether the need was for a large group or one individual, Jesus was alert to it. There is indeed a lesson herein for each of us. We are to be alert to the needs of others, be it a disenfranchised employee feeling marginalized, or a customer in need of our expertise.

Look at just a few biblical characters who took steps to make a difference, in some cases making an impact that would outlast their lifetime:

- Mary, visited by an angel and told she would conceive a baby even though she had never been intimate with a man, wasn't even married yet and had no idea what it would mean for her life and her future. Yet, in Luke 1:38 she trusted God and willingly committed to be part of something that would make a difference for the whole world and all people to come, responding "I am the Lord's servant." Little did she know what she was in for, including gut wrenching heartache, but she willingly took the risk to make a difference and stayed faithful to her commitment throughout her life.

- The first four disciples Jesus called were two sets of brothers (Peter and Andrew; James and John). They were fishermen, but Jesus said there were bigger needs that had to be met, thus they "left and followed Him," (Matthew 4:18-20) becoming disciples that would preach the Gospel and transform thousands of people into becoming Christians.

- Matthew was a tax collector, a position held in contempt much like some of our politicians and lawyers today. Jesus asked Matthew to leave his secure job and follow Him. (Mark 2:14) Unlike the fishermen who could have gone back to their jobs, Matthew was taking a substantial economic risk by leaving his job. Sensing life must have a greater purpose than financially greasing his own palms, he decided to follow Jesus. He later went on to author the first book of the New Testament.

- Joseph of Arimathea was a member of the Jewish council, the group that helped condemn Jesus. Joseph was a secret believer (John 19:38) but Jesus' death finally converted him once and for all. He risked his own reputation, stepped up and went to Pilate to get permission to meet a need, a place to bury the body of Jesus.

Business Practices, Biblical Promises

Contrast the above examples with the "leader" described as a ruler who came to Jesus and asked what he could do to make a difference. (Luke 18:18-24) Jesus told him to help the poor by selling his "stuff." The ruler walked away, sullen, because he did not like the answer Jesus gave him. He was more interested in acquiring and adding to his already impressive possession of assets, unwilling to give up the supposed security of his wealth.

Degrees and titles: no guarantee you'll be a good decision maker

Job titles, college or post-graduate degrees and prominent positions certainly can be of help, but they are no guarantee you or I will be true leaders, or professionals whose decisions make a substantive difference. Author Thomas Friedman, in an interview with Laszio Bock, Vice-President of People Operations of Google, quotes Bock in saying, "GPAs are worthless as a criteria for hiring, and test scores are worthless…we found that they don't predict anything. Beware. Your degree is not a proxy for your ability to do any job. The world only cares about—and pays off on—what you can do with what you know (and it doesn't care how you learned it). There is nothing wrong with good grades or degrees, but at Google they look at other things to determine a good hiring fit." [1]

Look at Jesus' disciples; we don't even know the former occupations of half of them. We know that five were fishermen and one was a tax collector. Yet they were willing to evaluate the evidence and the worthiness of the mission to be disciples. Upon their observation, experience and discernment, they poured themselves into their "jobs" with passion and preparedness (Acts 2). All but one were martyred for their work spreading the gospel; but, get this, we still talk about them in the 21st century. They changed the world and their impact continues.

Going back to Friedman's interview with Vice President Bock, one of their hiring criteria at Google "is leadership—in particular emergent leadership as opposed to traditional leadership. Traditional leadership is, were you president of the chess club? Were you vice president of sales? How quickly did you get there? At Google, they don't care. What they do care about is, when faced with a problem and you're a member of a team, do you, at the appropriate time, step in and lead?" Think about Michele versus her boss, Edward, in the opening story of this chapter.

Bock goes on to say "and just as critically, do you step back and stop leading, do you let someone else? Because what's critical to be an effective leader in this environment is you have to be willing to relinquish power." Think about Saul, the leader of Israel, when he decided to step back and let a young street-smart shepherd take the lead to make a difference in a military battle.

Along with the willingness to lead, Friedman further quotes Bock about humility and ownership: "…it's feeling the sense of responsibility, the sense of ownership to step in and to try to solve any problem—and the humility to step back and embrace the better ideas of others."[2] Think about Robin who held a fledging hospital together but stepped out by taking another job, leaving her employer once a full time executive was appointed to a role she likely could have done.

How do the foregoing stories apply to the life of a Christian business man or woman? We'll all face similar scenarios numerous times in our careers that require us to make a decision to step up, step back or step out in order to make a difference. Let's be honest, most leaders would first assess the risk-reward of what's in it for them. Christian leaders, however, have another filter to consider in their decision-making process. They need to ask themselves, "how do we act, react, or withhold action in a manner in which we can be a faithful disciple rather than a self-centered professional (like Edward in our opening story)?"

Our guiding example is Jesus. At times He stepped up and took action in numerous situations, such as the healing of the blind man, the feeding of large crowds, and His ultimate intervention of dying on the cross for our sins. At other times He stepped back—as he did, for example, when he sent his disciples out to preach in teams of two. (Mark 6: 7) Through His accession, He stepped out to conclude His earthly ministry, expecting all who are His disciples (in other words, all of us) to continue to spread the Gospel. (Mark 16: 15-20)

God does his work through "ordinary" people. You are part of His plan. A willingness to serve leads to making a difference. Making a difference will present opportunities for leadership. Becoming a leader presents the opportunity to multiply your impact.

So how does one know when to step up, step back, or step out?

The next three chapters will help prepare us to make wise God honoring decisions. The challenge: are *you* willing to make a difference, a difference that truly matters?

Chapter 1 Self-Assessment:
Are You Willing to Make a Difference?

Reflections:

1. Can you think of a time and place in which you were given the opportunity to step up and you made a difference?

2. Can you think of a time and place in which you were given the opportunity to step up and did not?

3. Have you ever experienced a situation like Saul where you stepped back?

4. Have you ever experienced a situation like Michele where you decided enough was enough, e.g., you changed jobs, or outright quit?

Action Steps:

1. If you answered "yes" to question one above:
    a. What made you step up?
    b. Did you consider your decision and action to be correct?
2. If you answered "yes" to question two, three or four above:
    a. What was the outcome?

      b. Would you make the same decision again?

      c. What might you do differently?

3. When you think about leadership, what specifically drives you to become a leader?

Key Bible Verse: Read and contemplate 1 Peter 5:2-4

Chapter 1: Footnotes

1. Thomas Friedman, "Only humble learners need apply at Google, *"Tampa Bay Times,"* (February 27, 2014): 11A.
2. Ibid.

Chapter 2
Talent, Teamwork and Training

While on a business trip flight, I had the privilege of sitting on the plane next to a former professional ice hockey player. He was a champion, with one of his teams twice winning the coveted Stanley Cup. Until speaking with him, I never realized what happened between his hockey playing days and his current occupation.

In our conversation he indicated that he had lost everything after his hockey career through several bad business decisions he made shortly after retiring from hockey. His restaurant business failed miserably. He was not a wealthy man, as hockey players tend to be paid less than athletes in other major sports. The humbling consequences of his business failure resulted in his declaring both personal and corporate bankruptcy, forcing him to sell his home, and even worse, it cost him his marriage. The only money he was able to retain was a few thousand dollars he stashed away.

But he took the little money he had, enrolled in acting classes and read everything he could about acting and communications. He started making money doing commercials. One of his first advertising gigs was for Hardee's Restaurants. He had one line to say, but that was the seed for future opportunity. He invested in developing his acting and communication talents and parlayed that into a three-part post-hockey career. In addition to being featured in many commercials over the years, he became a fine television hockey analyst in the USA and Canada. If that were not enough, the story of both his successes and failures has led him to be a sought after motivational speaker.[1] He learned that he did not just have one gift—that of a hockey player—but God in His Providence gave him even better gifts that he could use to reach more people through his work. His name is Bill Clement, a former member of the Philadelphia Flyers championship teams of the mid-1970's. I still remember seeing him while attending the Flyers Stanley Cup victory parades in Philly. The crowds were enormous. I still have the pictures to prove it.

The take-aways? First, it's never too late to develop your talent to make a difference. Doing so earlier in life may be preferable, but it is never too late, especially with the resources available in our internet age. The second point is that God has likely blessed you with more talents than you think you possess.

I serve on the board of a college in which most students are working adults. The average age of graduates at Peirce College is thirty-six. In a number of our June graduation ceremonies we have had multiple generations from the same family graduate together. Once we had a grandmother, mother and granddaughter walk across the stage the same evening to receive their college diplomas. It is literally never too late to take the time to gain the training or education needed to develop your God-given raw talent.

One's willingness to make a difference is essential; however, the talent we each bring to a role will significantly influence the impact we have as formal or informal leaders. Gretchen Pisano, one of two facilitators for the American Institute of Certified Public Accountants (AICPA) Leadership Academy, teaches that "leadership starts within. This process begins with a deep understanding of your strengths. What things come naturally to you? What things energize you?"[2]

All difference makers want to use their talent; however, as Christians we are encouraged to *fully* develop our gifts and talents to make ourselves available for God's complete purpose for our lives. (2 Timothy 1:6, 7) Business professionals who invest in fully developing their talents are in a position to make wiser decisions and expand the impact of those decisions.

The source of our talent

Understanding the source of your talent is critical to appreciating the kind of person you are and the influence you are capable of having on others. Some people spend years trying to figure out who they are. Therefore, this question of who you are is important to your internal peace and confidence. It will impact the decision making, interaction and difference you'll make with your family, community and business.

Some come to think they were born with wonderful talent, while others think they were short changed. Yet others believe they are simply the product of a great accidental cosmic bang that set off a chain of events in which, through evolutionary sequences, they came into being. I love science, and areas such as astronomy, geology, meteorology, etc., always interest me; however, my layman's view of evolution is that it takes more faith to buy into such a theory for our existence than deliberate creation.

Why is it important what we believe about our very being? As the authors of *Leading from Within* put it, "the knowledge of why we were made and what life really means creates a very different worldview for a leader…without a proper understanding of self and a sense of meaning and purpose, one cannot lead others."[3]

God gave you talent. He also gave specific talents to your co-workers, bosses, customers and clients. (Romans 12:6, 7) More importantly, God's Word, the Bible, is very clear about creation and purpose. He set out a plan before you and I were born onto this earth. Think about that for a moment. Let's look at a couple verses:

- "For you created my inmost being; you knit me together in my mother's womb. My frame was not hidden from you when I was made in a secret place, when I was woven together in the depths of the earth. Your eyes saw my unformed body; all the days ordained for me were written in your book before one of them came to be." (Psalm 139: 13, 15-16)

- "For by him all things were created: things in heaven and on earth, visible and invisible…all things were created by him and for him."

(Colossians 1: 16)

Amazing, isn't it, to think that God so detailed His marvelous creation that he had *you* in mind when he did all of this! Your existence is no accident.

Why is it important the use of our talents be tied to our spiritual worldview? Because, whoever one believes is the authority of one's life is foundational to his or her views on the big issues of life—relationships, business, money, power, etc. Is our authority God or ourselves? Our decisions will be shaped by the answer to this question.

A case in point is the business decisions made by a star professional football player, Mychal Kendricks. He was a member of the 2017 super bowl champion Philadelphia Eagles, later traded to the Cleveland Browns in early 2018. He had worked hard from the age of five to develop and become an outstanding player. But in his words he "wanted to be more than just a football player."

So he put his trust in a friend who had previous work experience and professional contacts at the investment banking firm of Goldman Sachs. His "friend" gave him inside information on companies that were planning to merge so that Mr. Kendricks could invest and profit from this knowledge. He in turn used his position of influence to provide his friend with cash and perks as a reward for this information, which profited Mr. Kendricks over one million dollars from just four transactions.

His views on relationships (a friend he thought he could trust); money (more and easy); business (be more than a football player); and power (used his position to provide game tickets in return for more favors), all converged, leading to decisions reflective of who and what was important in his life.

When the scheme was publicly exposed in August of 2018, he admitted that though he did not fully understand the legality of insider trading rules, he nevertheless knew it was wrong. The day following this public announcement, Mychal was released from the Cleveland Browns and currently faces legal charges that could lead to significant time in prison. Indeed our spiritual worldview as to who is the authority of our life will determine who and what is important, greatly influencing the decisions we make. [4]

When we think what we have accomplished or acquired in life is the sole product of our own doing and talent, think about this admonition paraphrased from Isaiah 22: 7-11: "Your choicest mode of transportation is luxury cars; your home is guarded by a gated community; you saved up money; you counted your assets and investment portfolio, you stripped down or sold businesses to make bigger and better profits; but you did not look to the One who made it or have regard for the One who planned it long ago."

Mychal Kendricks and numerous other business professionals have learned this admonition the hard way.

It's easy to leave God out of the process when things are going well. Re-read those verses from Isaiah 22:7-11 and see the warning of that era remains relevant to our time.

Business Practices, Biblical Promises

You were cast for a purpose.

When God created us, He also gave each of us certain talents, or gifts, that are unique to the purpose He intended for us. "To some He gives the gift of teaching, others prophets (think advisors, consultants); others the gift of healing (think doctors, nurses, counselors); others the gifts of help and encouragement; and some the gifts of administration and leadership…" (1 Corinthians 12: 27, 28; Romans 12:6-8) There are different kinds of gifts needed to serve and perform work, but it is God who bestowed on each of us our talent. (1 Corinthians 12: 4, 5)

If you are having trouble discerning your particular gift(s) or talent(s), any number of professionally administered tests can aid you. The Strong Interest Inventory and the Myers Briggs personality test are two such examples.

Well into my adult life a Sunday school teacher administered such a test. He was a middle-aged man whose teaching abilities garnered the attention of the classroom comprised of adult couples in our modest-sized Methodist Church in Clearwater, Florida. Upon my taking the test, something I enjoyed doing but never recognized as a gift emerged: the gift of giving.

Once identified, I was able to become more deliberate and intentional with my giving beyond tithing to our local church, and it became even more enjoyable. For example, as God blessed our consulting company with work in various parts of the country, my wife and I would choose a Christian school in that area and seek to sponsor a child who, absent financial assistance, would not be able to obtain a Christian education. It was one way of giving back to those communities where God had blessed our company with work. Once again it is *never* too late to discover and develop your talent.

Your gifts are not just for your own use and benefit. In our work place we are usually part of a team. We are more effective team members if we know when to step up, step back, or step out. Webster's dictionary describes teamwork as "work done by several associates with each doing a part but all subordinating personal prominence to the efficiency of the whole." [5] In other words, our God given gifts are to be used to help others, be it in the workplace or in service outside our place of business..

As the book of Romans expresses, "For just as each of us has one body with many members, and these members do not all have the same function, so in Christ we, though many, form one body, and each member belongs to all the others." (Romans 12: 4,5).

Here is a story from the Bible that illustrates this concept. (You could likely substitute the name of someone you know for Moses or perhaps use your own name and it will still ring true today). Moses was called by God to lead the people of Israel out of Egypt around 1450 BC. When God gave Moses this leadership challenge, Moses responded that he was not qualified, as he was not eloquent; he did not speak well…in fact he stuttered. I for one can relate to this as I have a fear, bordered on dread, of public speaking and I suspect most of you can also relate. God responded to Moses asking who gave him his mouth, as God promised he would help him. Moses' response to this is stunning: "Lord, please send someone else." (Exodus 4:10-13) Moses certainly had no willingness to make a difference for God's people at that moment of his life! God was incredibly patient with Moses in his reluctance to step up. In order to provide him some comfort, given his intimidation, he teamed Moses with Aaron who was bestowed with the gift of public speaking. (Exodus 4: 14-16)

We were created to live in community with others, meaning that, in order to be most effective in carrying out God's Plan, you need the gifts and talents of other people to complement your own just as your talents complement and assist others. None of us has a corner on talent. We all have areas where we need additional help to carry out our purpose in business and in life. Peter Drucker, the well-respected 20th century business philosopher and educator, states "management is about human beings. Its task is to make people capable of joint performance, to make their strengths effective and their weaknesses irrelevant."[6]

God often uses what we see as ordinary people to do extraordinary things (no one is ordinary in God's eyes; it is our own human pride or egotistical view of ourselves that misleads us to think that).

In an amazing story told in Judges Chapters 6-8, a man named Gideon becomes immersed in his job, basically trying to survive and feed his family, working very hard in an agriculture business. His people, the Israelites, had once again turned from God and as a consequence were being ruled by a group of people called Midianites. They, along with other eastern peoples, would routinely invade the parcels of land occupied by the Israelites and ravage their food and animals.

God called upon Gideon to lead a military challenge to basically take out their biggest oppressor. Many of us can probably think of a business competitor we would love to see defeated, or at least diminished. Gideon had his doubts about this mission since it was quite a stretch from the way his talent was being used. But God creatively presents opportunities to stretch us, if we allow Him. Such opportunities are usually presented when we are using our gifts faithfully and to the fullest in our current challenge or assignment. So, even if the leadership role presented to Gideon happened to make any sense to him, he certainly felt inadequate to do it.

But God worked through all of his doubts and questions and stretched his talent to do things he could not ever have dreamed were possible. Gideon led an army of three hundred to defeat the Midianites' army of thousands. God intentionally demonstrated that His power means more than whether a business has more or less of something, be it size or money.

If you think this idea of a person going from agricultural work into the military field is a far-fetched story, some readers will remember our country use to have a military draft. You could be a student, farmer or businessman one day and the very next day you were in the military; and, shortly thereafter you could easily be the

Business Practices, Biblical Promises

leader of a squad or platoon and find yourself immersed in a military battle in a place like Vietnam.

In my first career job I took a leave of absence from a large certified public accounting firm on a Friday and the following week was in basic infantry training for the Army National Guard in Fort Polk, Louisiana. The point is, God is looking for "ordinary" people—like you—who are willing to be stretched and accomplish great things you probably have never even considered you could or would do before! God has a purpose for each of us.

I'm sure you have met people whose talent did not seem to fit into your unit or company. From their point of view, they likely did not feel appreciated in their own organization. I remember an instance in my career when a few individuals felt ostracized from the main stream of our organization, being excluded from key meetings and informal discussions. As a result, they formed their own team so that they had some sense of belonging. Looking back, we did a poor job of integrating them into the main team. People who want to make a difference make a wise decision by helping other people achieve their potential.

The Bible tells the story of a man who did not seem to fit in. His name was Jephthah, a "mighty warrior," extraordinary in his role (Judges 11: 1), however, he was ostracized because he came from a blended family. In his case his birth mother was a prostitute, not a good social position for his career advancement. Jephthah felt so out of place he left and went to a different "company." He quickly developed a following as they appreciated the superior level of talent he brought to their organization. And if you think the Bible is not relevant to today, Jephthah's former clan (think company) later sought him out for the purpose of recruiting him back to take the leadership role in trying to topple their leading "competitor."

Jephthah is evidence that sometimes a person's talents are not appreciated until he or she leaves an organization. You probably can relate to this, perhaps in a very personal way. But what should be comforting is that our social position or physical limitations don't necessarily have to hold us back or stand in the way of us using our God-given talent, as Jephthah demonstrates. Jephthah committed to honing his skills despite cultural and social challenges. As the Psalmist said "He raises the poor from the dust and lifts the needy from the ash heap; he seats them with princes." (Psalm 113:7-8)

There is no question we all have been blessed with God-given talent. The question is, what are we doing to develop and hone our gifts so that our decisions have the most effective impact?

The quality of your purpose depends on you!

What you do with your talent to help others and honor God is up to you. This in itself is a milestone decision impacting your life and career.

Whether or not you believe you were created by God, you're being in this place and moment in time in itself is a gift that has been given to you. In 2 Corinthians 3:5 the apostle Paul makes it clear that "our competence comes from God."

Business Practices, Biblical Promises

However, there are numerous talented people who, frankly, are not successful; we have all met such people. We need to educate, train and discipline ourselves to develop our gifts in order to fully utilize the talent for which God has created us. As John Wooden, the former and famous basketball coach at UCLA says, "failing to prepare is preparing to fail."[7]

Thus we must be willing to invest in developing our talent. One can go to college and come home not having done much to actually cultivate talent. To quote Thomas Fuller, "if an ass goes traveling, he'll not come home a horse."[8] Traveling is an activity, going back and forth is an activity, but "investing" involves time, study, money, experience, testing, failing, getting up, stretching yourself, keeping at it, getting better and better—one decision, project or job at a time.

As leadership coach, author and clinical psychologist Dr. Henry Cloud puts it, "the question is more about this: are you only achieving average results in relation to where you or your business are supposed to be? In other words, given your abilities, resources, and opportunities, are you reaching your full potential? Or are you drifting toward a middle that is lower than where you should be if you were getting the most from what you are and what you have?"[9]

We are strongly encouraged to "fan the flame of the gift of God" (2 Timothy 1:6), meaning we are to use fully our God given talent, and do so wisely.

King Solomon wanted to build a temple, but he clearly needed more experienced workers to accomplish this significant project. In Chronicles 2, Chapter 2, Solomon asked the King of Tyre for an expert. The King sent a man named Huram-Abi as an independent contractor or consultant.

Read this description of a man who truly had invested in honing his talent:

> *He is trained to work in gold and silver, bronze and iron, stone and wood, and with purple and blue and crimson yarn and fine linen. He is experienced in all kinds of engraving and can execute any design given to him. He will work with your skilled workers.* (2 Chronicles 2:14)

Huram-Abi was trained and experienced, plus, like any good leader, he would teach Solomon's own craftsmen and pass on what he had learned. Achieving this level of competence took years of trials, experience, and a substantial investment in time. Again, you don't need a fancy title to make a difference. This was a man who honed his talent so well that he was brought into Solomon's country to lead other craftsmen. His story should inspire each of us to fully invest in enhancing our talent.

Education and training: a life journey

Continuing education is a lifelong pursuit which leaders should practice and encourage others to do so as well. I am most grateful for my own college education; but, without a doubt, most of my learning has been acquired post-college through reading, studying, observing, failing, experimenting and practicing, as well as enrolling in formal continuing education classes. As Chuck Lauer, former publisher of *Modern Healthcare* says regarding true leadership,

Business Practices, Biblical Promises

"effective leaders don't stop learning. They read, they listen to others and they go to seminars and meetings—all to stay on top of new concepts and knowledge."[10]

Education and training take *purposeful* time, study and practice. "Teaching" requires both a willing, caring and capable teacher, and a very willing learner and listener. To illustrate this point, one of my most profound experiences occurred in a continuing education setting. This was not your usual "sit back in class and mark off eight hours of continuing education by enduring the day." This was an intense, interactive, five-day work session of forty classroom hours.

On day two, the instructor dismissed one of the class participants. What we students did not know was that the instructor observed the immaturity of this participant and privately warned her after day one. On day two, observing no change, the instructor decided that her own reputation as an instructor and the success of the class overall was more important than taking a fee from a person who was simply not teachable. It was a sobering experience to see a fellow student dismissed. The instructor's action of protecting the learning environment for the participants engendered respect and increased attentiveness from all of us.

The Bible asks us to "apply your heart to instruction and your ears to words of knowledge." (Proverbs 23: 12) Think of Jesus' disciples and the investment they made over three years before they were ready to fully use what they had learned. They were willing to learn the Lord's way; they were teachable.

In another New Testament story we see a husband and wife

team, Aquila and Priscilla, who used their home for teaching, training and evangelism. (Acts 18: 18-28) On one occasion, a person named Apollos had great zeal and enthusiasm but was not sufficiently grounded in principles and facts. We all have met people full of zeal but lacking in practical training and experience. Aquila and Priscilla took time to train Apollos, as he was teachable. He later demonstrated what a good student he was as he vigorously engaged in debate "proving from the Scriptures that Jesus was the Messiah." (Acts 18:28)

Paul, the great New Testament missionary, had the training and experience that later led to an incredible opportunity in Athens to debate with the leading philosophers. How many people would be willing to do that? Paul was a rabbi who went to Tarsus, then an educational center, and was trained by one of the finest scholars of the day, Gamaliel. He was well prepared and sufficiently knowledgeable to engage a group of philosophers. (Acts 17: 16-34.)[11] Paul understood that developing talent requires discipline.

He expressed this in his writings to the Church of Corinth when he compared his work to an athletic competition: "Do you not know that in a race all the runners run, but only one gets the prize? Run in such a way as to get the prize. Everyone who competes in the games goes into strict training. They do it to get a crown that will not last, but we do it to get a crown that will last forever." (1 Corinthians 9: 24, 25)

"Running to get the prize" and "strict training" came into

focus for me when I had to prepare for a certification exam in healthcare financial management. We know not everyone will get first place, or a top prize, but we prepare as if that is our aim, we want to do our best. So in my study for the certification examination I put together a study plan as if I was shooting for the top prize. I certainly had no realistic expectation of achieving it, I simply wanted my preparation to be such that I could pass the exam on the first try and avoid waiting a year for a do-over along with investing in even more study time. You see, the year before I had cut corners in studying for the CPA exam and had to take one of the four parts over again. By aiming for the top this time, I was hoping to "finish," that is, pass that exam. I did not want to repeat, so I went into "strict training," or studying. The Lord blessed me beyond my wildest dreams when I indeed achieved the top national score on that year's certification and achieved Fellow status in healthcare financial management.

More important, however, than professional recognition, Paul further states in his letter to Timothy, is to "train yourself to be godly. For physical training is of some value, but godliness has value for all things, holding promise for both the present life and the life to come." (1 Timothy 4: 7, 8)

As decision makers who aspire to please God first and foremost we are to further train ourselves in the scriptures, be discerning and growing in God's word, and thus become prepared for moments of opportunity to serve or lead. (Hebrews 5: 11-14; 6:1-3) As the apostle

Peter wrote in one of his letters, we are to "always be prepared to give an answer to everyone who asks you to give the reason for the hope that you have. But do this with gentleness and respect." (1 Peter 3:15)

Dr. Ben Carson, in his book, *One Nation,* cites a speech by Dr. Martin Luther King, Jr., in which the renowned civil rights leader stated that Jesus Christ was the best example of someone who overcame less than optimistic circumstances considering his parents had no social standing or wealth in that generation. He states that "not environment, not heredity, but personal response is the final determining factor in our lives. And herein lies our area of responsibility."[12]

We need to prepare ourselves through formal education or training, self-education, and experiences that will enhance our skill sets and character. In fact, Dr. Carson recounts that he can look back on every job he ever held and see that some aspect of each of those varied and often low paying experiences became a building block toward his career as a world-renowned pediatric neurosurgeon.[13]

How and where to use your talent?

Assuming our willingness to step up to make a difference by developing our gifts, we must then decide how and where we choose to use our time and talent.

Jesus made a point about the appropriate use of our talent and business enterprise in a rather dramatic display. While in Jerusalem

Business Practices, Biblical Promises

He found business being conducted in the temple. Jesus made an example of those entrepreneurs by effectively shutting them down. This action imparted two messages: one, it let them know that where their business was being conducted was inappropriate and two, it revealed that a number of the businesses were simply dishonest, regardless of their location. (Matthew 21:12, 13) If where and how we use our talent was important to Jesus it ought to be important to us. This raises several practical questions:

- How did you choose to work where you are right now? Why?
- Are you working in a business selling or making a product or service that is both legal and ethical?
- Can you honor God in this business?
- If you had to choose your current work over again, would you?
- If you lost your current job or your company went out of business tomorrow, where or how would you then choose to use your time and talent?

None of us wants to get to the end of our career and think we spent time in something that provided no real or lasting value, or that perhaps we forfeited other more appropriate opportunities to make a difference. We go through seasons of life. We change and companies around us change; new ones are formed, other companies disappear, while existing companies try to figure out how to thrive or survive. Be deliberate on where and how you are using your capabilities.

Your decision on how and where you use your talent is consequential given a majority of your life will (hopefully) be spent using it. If you have truly invested in recognizing and developing your gifts, you are not trapped—you have choices—and remember it's never too late to seek additional training and education. Will the business and career decisions you make enable the Lord to say "Well done, good and faithful servant?" (Matthew 25:21) These words, His words, should guide us on how and where we choose to use our God given talent.

Your talent is not about you, it is God given. What you do with your talent is about you. That decision will determine the depth, breadth and quality of your service and its impact on family, friends, colleagues, company, customers, and your life. In conclusion, reflect on this verse penned by Roy Lessin, the co-founder of Day Spring Cards:

Just think

You're here not by chance but by God's choosing.
His hand formed you and made you the person you are.
He compares you to no one else—you are one of a kind.
You lack nothing that His grace can't give you.
He has allowed you to be here at this time in history
To fulfill His special purpose for this generation.[14]

Chapter 2 Self-Assessment:
Talent, Teamwork and Training

Reflections:

1. Do you believe God blessed you with talent?
2. Do you know what primary or secondary gifts you have?
3. Have you fully invested in developing your talent?
4. Do you have a sense of purpose for your life?

Action Steps:

1. God doesn't usually bless us with promotions unless we are fully utilizing our talent in our current role. Are you fully utilizing your gifts and talents? Write a paragraph or two to answer this question.
2. This exercise will provide initial insight into your purpose and talent. Answer the following:
    a. What do you believe comes naturally to you?
    b. What projects or type of work have you most enjoyed?
    c. What volunteer work have you most enjoyed?
    d. What are your three most memorable accomplishments? Be specific. What made them so?
    e. If you knew money were no issue and you knew you could not fail, what would you do?

f. Do you believe your talent is being best used where you are now?
3. Are you working in an organization in which its service or product places you in a position to honor God? If not, consider a change.
   a. God wants to stretch you. Ask yourself: How many hours have you invested in self-improvement or continuing education in the last twelve months?
   b. Do you need additional formal education or technical training to be completely useful and available for God to use your talents?
   c. Consider hiring a career coach or some other professional to assist you in taking steps to further discover and/or develop your God given talent.

Key Bible Verses: Read and consider 1 Corinthians 9: 24-27; Romans 12: 6-8; 2 Timothy 1:6.

Chapter 2: Footnotes

1. Bill Clement, *Everyday Leadership, Crossing Gorges on Tightropes to Success,* (Self-Published by WHC Enterprises, 2011), pp. 141-160; 179,180.
2. Dan Griffiths, CPA, CGMA, "The Leading Edge," *Journal of Accountancy* (July 2014), p. 53.

3. Thomas E. Beeman and Richard Glenn, *Leading from Within,* (Franklin, Tennessee: Providence House Publishers, 2005), pp. 6-7.
4. Scott Calvert and Andrew Beaton, "NFL Player Charged in Insider-Trading Case," *The Wall Street Journal,* (August 30., 2018), p. B10.
5. Merriam-Webster's Collegiate Dictionary, 2014 (Merriam-Webster, Inc., Springfield, Massachusetts) p. 1282
6. Peter F. Drucker, *The New Realities,* (New York: Harper & Row, 1989), p. 229.
7. Goodreads.com, "John Wooden Quotes." (http://www.goodreads.com/author/quotes/23041. John Wooden). (accessed September 19, 2014).
8. Goodreads.com, "Thomas Fuller Quotes. (http://www.goodreads.com/author/quotes/433477.Thomas_Fuller?p=2. (accessed September 19, 2014)
9. Dr. Henry Cloud, *Necessary Endings*, (New York: Harper Collins, 2010), p. 19.
10. Chuck Lauer, "What Makes a Great Mentor: 10 Traits of True Leadership," (http://www.beckershospitalreview.com/hospital-management-administration/what-makes-a-great-mentor-10-traits-of-true-leadersip.html), November 7, 2012. (accessed April 23, 2018).

11. Acts 17, *Life Application Bible,* New International Version, (Tyndale House, Wheaton, Illinois, and Zondervan Grand Rapids, Michigan, 1991), p. 1996.
12. Ben Carson with Candy Carson, *One Nation*, (New York: Sentinel, Penguin Group, 2014), pp. 42-43
13. Ibid., pp. 158-160.
14. Goodreads.com, "Roy Lessin Quotes." (http://www.goodreads.com/author/quotes/376074.Roy_Lessin). (accessed September 19, 2014).

Chapter 3
Making Wise Decisions: Heart Matters

In the early 1980's I was promoted to become the Chief Executive Officer (CEO) of a community hospital in Lancaster County, Pa. I had lived outside the county where this hospital was located, but with my new role I was compelled to move within the town limits. With increased responsibilities at work along with raising a young family, I felt considerable pressure to sell our house at a time when interest rates were eighteen percent. Some readers will remember that recession era: a period of high inflation, a housing crisis, and long lines at gasoline filling stations.

One evening the realtor came to our house to present an offer. The buyer asked for an installment sale, a transaction which would take three years to completely consummate. I signed the offer. Such sales were not uncommon at that time; "creative financing" was the way to close real estate transactions in that difficult economy.

I could not sleep that night. My stomach was in knots. I tried to come to grips with the decision I had made the previous evening. During a restless night in bed I prayed for God's help, realizing I should have been praying *before* I signed the contract. I knew I made an impulsive decision. I wasn't even totally sure what truly comprised an installment sale. I hadn't requested nor taken the time to investigate the facts. As I thought more about what I had done, I realized I made a terrible financial decision. Furthermore, I wasn't even sure moving my family closer to my place of work was the right decision for them or even for me.

In this particular situation God was indeed merciful. I called the realtor early in the morning and asked her if she had presented our signed contract to the buyer. She had not. I asked her to rip up the papers; we were not going forward with the transaction.

I dodged a financial bullet, one of my own making. I had not made a good business decision in signing that contract. I simply had not done the homework to even be in a position of making a wise decision. The homework required for wise decisions is a matter of both the heart and mind. In this chapter we'll focus on how heart matters contribute to making God-honoring decisions.

Wisdom: *What is it and how do we get it?*

Wisdom is first a choice. The Bible says that wisdom is available to all of us, (Proverbs 8:1) but it must be chosen. Just as the gift of eternal salvation through acceptance of Jesus into our hearts is universally available to all, it must be individually accepted. (John 3:16) Consider these words from the Bible, "Choose my instruction instead of silver, knowledge rather than choice gold, for wisdom is more precious than rubies and nothing you desire can compare to her." (Proverbs 8:10,11) Wisdom is available to us for guidance in life, including our work life, but seeking it is a choice we individually make. I wasn't seeking wisdom when I signed the real estate offer, I just wanted the move behind me.

What is wisdom? *Wisdom is making decisions by assessing the potential impact of our action or restraint from action from the point of view of how God instructs us to live.* Wisdom is spiritually discerned. It is using information, observations, experiences and circumstances to assess situations as God might have us view them. We, of course, are not God, but He has given us His word, the Bible, to guide us in our businesses and in our lives.

Since wisdom is a choice and is spiritually discerned, how do we get it? As it pertains to matters of the heart, we must make an internal assessment in three areas: reverence, prayer and obedience. It all starts with a willingness to follow God's preferred way of conducting business.

Reverence for God

The Bible clearly states the "the fear of the Lord is the beginning of wisdom." (Psalm 111: 10a; Proverbs 1:7; 9:10) A prerequisite for wisdom is reverence for God, it's our first step. God created us for fellowship with Him, but He gives us the choice to engage in it. We can serve Him, ourselves, or something or someone else. Reverence is our first step toward making wise decisions. Right thinking requires thinking right about God.

"Wisdom's instruction is to fear the Lord, and humility comes before honor." (Proverbs 15:33) Some leaders seem to think enjoyment in life is compromised by deference or respect to God. Quite to the contrary, in a world where we are so busy acquiring, building and buying, many people have little contentment. "The fear of the Lord leads to life, then one rests content." (Proverbs 19:23) In other words, we can work through the circumstances that crush most people by making choices that honor God above all. If we make decisions as if there is no God (or as if we are gods), we'll never truly be content.

Prayer: *'Like I have time for that?'*

Does prayer have a place in the decision-making processes of our professional lives? Do leaders with demanding schedules really have time to pray? After all, difference makers are extremely busy, paid to achieve results, thus we're under pressure to make timely decisions.

Nehemiah was a great Old Testament leader who had a bold vision and goals for a project he wanted to accomplish which he thought would make a difference in the lives of many people. He wanted to rebuild a city, Jerusalem. But the very first action he took was to pray. (Nehemiah 1:4) We'll talk several times throughout this book about him because he exemplifies a person who made wise business decisions. Similarly, King David prayed to know the truth and the right path to take. (Psalm 25:4, 5)

Prayer is communicating with God, giving us access to His grace. Business people know the importance of communicating with the boss. When we gain access to the boss we receive information and direction that helps us carry out our responsibilities. If we don't effectively communicate (present, ask, listen), things can get off course. It's the same with our relationship with a spouse or significant other—if we don't effectively communicate, we'll soon wish we had! Praying (communicating) with God is key to our decision making.

When Jesus conducted his earthly ministry He was as busy as any one leader could be with people constantly wanting a piece of His time and energy. (Luke 5:15, 16; Mark 1:35-37) Some people wanted His time and energy because they genuinely needed His help, healing and guidance; others wanted His attention because they were seeking a benefit for their own self-centered agenda; still others literally wanted a piece of Jesus because they sought to thwart His goals and end his career. Many leaders can relate to these three different kinds of pressures Jesus faced.

Regardless of these constant pressures, Jesus made prayer a priority and took time to pray, often getting up early in the morning to do so. (Mark 1:35) Prayer was not only a priority for Jesus, it was a significant priority. His disciples noticed. They could have asked Jesus for just about anything but they specifically asked Him to teach them how to pray. (Luke 11:1) This should be a take-away for all of us. Why should leaders pray? Why should anyone pray? Why pray *before* making decisions? Here are five reasons for making prayer, a matter of the heart, a priority:

1. Prayer is powerful and effective (James 5:16) even if we don't know it.

I had a client who offered me the job of being their company's chief financial officer. I really enjoyed the company's staff, and its geographic location was interesting to me. Most importantly, it meant I could get off the road and spend much more time with my family. I was so close to taking that job my wife and I began looking at houses. But as I continued to pray about this offer I had uneasiness in my heart. Finally, I realized it centered on my lack of trust in the executive who would be my boss. I turned the job down and stayed with my employer. Little did I know that several years later my bosses would ask me to run their company and I'd have a chance to own part of it. Prayer makes a difference beyond our understanding because God is beyond our comprehension. (Job 36:26)

Even if the outcomes of our prayers are not what we would have preferred, prayer gives us the strength to endure uncertain or difficult circumstances. God works out the big picture of human dynamics which is beyond what we can appreciate during our short time on this earth. (Romans 8:28)

2. Prayer helps us remember we are not alone.

All of us have experienced loneliness in our careers. Leadership responsibilities can especially leave us feeling lonely at times. We get frustrated that others don't understand the demands of time and multiple priorities. But God urges us to take comfort, He is in charge, we are not alone. (Psalm 118:6-9) In fact a salient test of our own leadership and maturity is what we do when we are alone.

Praying brings us back to a sense that life is not about us. God in his providence places us in positions providing opportunities to serve and impact others. The question again becomes who are we serving? Prayer gives us that sense of priority and reminds us that we can't control most things in life; however, He, who knows all things, is with us at all times, we are never alone. (Matthew 28:20)

3. Praying for others is a Biblical responsibility.

At one time I attended a church where the congregation on Sunday mornings was made up of about five-hundred worshippers. Missionaries who were home on furlough would sometimes slip into the church service after being away for three or four years. During the course of his sermon the pastor would uncannily spot these missionaries, stop his sermon and greet the returning missionaries by name. People were always amazed at his ability to spot faces and recall names. Early in my own tenure at this church while walking along a corridor the pastor greeted me by name. I was taken back, figuring there was no way he could possibly know me.

Upon his retirement the "secret" to his memory was disclosed. He prayed for each and every member of the congregation. People who became members had their pictures taken. Each week he would take a certain number of pictures with their corresponding names and pray for that segment of the membership, memorizing the name associated with the picture. It taught me a great lesson. At that time I was a CEO of a hospital. My pastor's example inspired me to do something similar, though admittedly not to the same degree as my pastor.

Another leader enjoyed lighting a candle for each of her clients. Though not Catholic, she liked the ritual and visual reminder of each client, and while she was in prayerful meditation, helpful ideas on their behalf would come to her mind.[1] Praying for our fellow workers, clients and customers places the purpose of our business and career in its proper context.

The beautiful and moving words of Jesus praying for His management team, His disciples, is a must read for every leader. (John 17: 6-19) We are also commanded to pray for those in authority over us. (1 Timothy 2:1) Do you pray for your team and your bosses (Hebrews 13:7)?

4. Prayer is an opportunity to ask God, not omit Him.

The Bible instructs us to bring *all* concerns to God (1 Peter 5:7) and devote ourselves to prayer. (Colossians 4:2) At times in our own confidence, self-assuredness, or even arrogance we make decisions on matters seemingly obvious, not in need of the advice of a "higher power."

God knows our needs and desires, but He enjoys when we ask for what our heart desires. "You do not have, because you do not ask God." (James 4:2b) The key is asking with an honest motive as we seek to make the wisest business decisions. God knows our heart.

The great Old Testament leader Joshua and his management team made a strategic alliance without praying for God's guidance on the matter. (Joshua Chapter 9) They did not pray nor perform due diligence in checking out a group of people known as the Gibeonites who initiated the request for a treaty. Later, upon learning the business deal was based on deception, it caused great consternation. In this case Joshua and the Israelites had to live with a deal they would have never consummated if they had known it was against God's will. They failed to pray and check out the facts of the situation, taking only their competitor's word. But the deal had been sealed and would not be undone. There are indeed consequences to leaving God out of our decision making.

5. Prayer helps us count our blessings.

Business is very competitive, life is tough and at times seems unfair from our human point of view. When we meditate and consider our circumstances we realize many blessings are bestowed upon us we often take for granted. Jesus took the time to give thanks *before* the outcome was known to those around Him, be it the feeding of multitudes of people, or the individual act of raising Lazarus from the dead.

Consider this observation by another leader:

> *"We have been the recipients of the choicest bounties of Heaven; we have been preserved these many years, in peace and prosperity; we have grown in numbers, wealth and power as no nation has ever grown. But we have forgotten God. We have forgotten the gracious hand which preserves us in the peace, and multiplied and enriched and strengthened us; and we have vainly imagined in the deceitfulness of our hearts that all these blessings were produced by some superior wisdom and virtue of our own."*

This was part of the proclamation made by President Abraham Lincoln in 1863 when he declared the first Thanksgiving in America, a day of "humiliation, fasting, and prayer." The outcome of the civil war was unknown when Lincoln called on the nation to pray and give thanks for its blessing. [2]

Business Practices, Biblical Promises

Making a business successful is very hard work. Having spent the second half of my career leading three consulting firms of varying sizes I came to appreciate that no matter how big or small our company was, we were always three months away from being out of business, running out of cash. I was thankful to God for the blessing of working with colleagues whose collective talents allowed us to compete and win our share of work and help our clients. There is much to be thankful for in having work to do, let alone other blessings in our life. Take the time to think more specifically about your blessings and thank Him daily.

Obedience to God's Word

We want to make the "right" decision. We want to make wise decisions. Christians desire to know God's will. Finding God's will is not searching for a point in the sky or a needle in a haystack, its not one thing. Just as a soccer field or football field has a wide span of play, it also has boundaries for which to guide the activity of the players. God gives us considerable freedom within the boundaries. Remember, God gave Adam and Eve incredible freedom, only asking they not eat from the tree of the knowledge of good and evil, which unfortunately they choose to do. The rules of play are found in the Bible.

So, in our pursuit of wisdom, the next heart matter we need to honestly confront is our willingness to *obey* God's rules of play for business and life. This is difficult at times, but a loving God designed us for fellowship with Him. He provides guidance not only for our own well-being, but for all those we interact with in our daily lives. If you need a little inspiration about the importance of this step consider these words: "Do not forget my teaching, but keep my commands in your heart, for they will prolong your life many years and bring you prosperity." (Proverbs 3:1, 2) We are instructed to "guard" His teachings and write them on the tablets of our hearts. (Proverbs 7: 2,3)

How do we do this? First, set time aside time to read the Bible, pray and ponder what has been read, and then consider how it might apply to your life. What practical action steps can you take to live a God honoring life? What do you need to do? Are their activities or habits you need to stop? Others you need to start? Make Bible reading and study a priority and do it consistently. Consistency demonstrates it is a priority and you will be the wiser for it.

Second, try to memorize scripture. The memorization of passages that touch your life will come back many times to help you in decision making as you recall portions of God's Word "written in your heart." Memorization of scripture fosters our obedience to God, especially when timely or difficult decisions need to be made.

I think one of the most profound blessings in my life as a teenager was the encouragement of pastors, Sunday school teachers, and youth leaders to memorize scripture. I remember not long after becoming a Christian, our Sunday school teacher wanted us to memorize the names of the books of the Bible and know the spelling of each.

Business Practices, Biblical Promises

Back in those days (1960's) we played sandlot baseball with pick-up games after school and then every day during the summer. Our Sunday school teacher would give out prizes for the top three winners in the Bible book spelling contest: a baseball glove, a bat and a ball. How I wanted to win one of those prizes! I did my best to memorize the names and spelling of the sixty-six books of the Bible. I won third prize, the baseball. I missed out winning the entire contest in a rather ironic manner as I correctly spelled "Thessalonians," but somehow missed on the spelling of the much simpler book, "Timothy." I remember it like it was yesterday.

Through the guidance and encouragement of these local church leaders I would memorize verses and passages of the Bible. One year I won a vacation Bible school contest in part because I could recite the twelfth chapter of Romans verse by verse, word for word. I only mention this for of the following two reasons:

First, memorization has enabled me to recall the scriptures during moments while facing challenges and opportunities in my work and personal life. These memorized scriptures provided wisdom in key times and moments. For example, I have led various companies which at times attracted interest from other organizations wanting to merge or buy us. Recalling a verse such as "do not be yoked together with unbelievers" (2 Corinthians 6:14) has served me well in business, as it counsels us against forming alliances with those whose values might cause us to compromise our faith. Mergers that fail are often due to disparate cultures. Merger and acquisition experts would be wise to learn just how much the Bible has to say about alliances.

The second reason I use these personal examples is because my only regret is not having memorized more scripture. Consider the Reverend Billy Graham who wrote a book three years before passing away in February of 2018 at the age of ninety-nine titled *Where I Am: Heaven, Eternity and Our Life Beyond*. It was about how faith grows when one is deliberate in learning from the Scriptures. He said, "I am thankful to have committed much of God's Word to memory."

In an age in which the Bible is being marginalized in our society, inspire yourself and others, such as your family and close business associates, to be in God's Word. Doing so will help you keep another command in seeking wisdom: that is "above all else, guard your heart, for everything you do flows from it. Keep your mouth free of perversity; keep corrupt talk far from your lips. Let your eyes look straight ahead; be steadfast in all your ways. (Proverbs 4: 23-25a, 26b)

In seeking God's wisdom, a litmus test Jesus gave us in terms of our commitment to following Him is "for where your treasure is, there your heart will be also." (Luke 12:34) We each must ask what is it that we really treasure? Jesus wants our hearts. He blesses those who desire to obey Him.

Our thought process in contemplating decisions should be like that of King Solomon who succeeded his father David as king of Israel. When God said to Solomon, "Ask for whatever you want me to give to you," (1 Kings 3:5) he responded "give your servant a discerning heart to govern your people and to distinguish between right and wrong." (1 Kings 3:9)

Knowing right from wrong requires being familiar with God's business and life manual, the Bible. The more we read and study it the more we understand God's perspective and can make wiser decisions. An important caveat: God will not honor decisions and actions that are contrary to His Word, so being immersed in the Bible is critical to making wise decisions.

We live at a time where ideological alignment, safe zones and fake news increasingly become defining factors in decision making; however, our desire to obey God should inspire us toward a faithful pursuit for truth, and to seek truth from a heart of love. The fundamental key to making wise decisions is to be sure your heart is aligned with God's preferred way to live.

What is that way? Jesus summarized all the commandments and laws into two:

"Love the Lord with all your heart and with all your soul and with all your mind and with all your strength. The second is this: 'Love your neighbor as yourself.' There is no commandment greater than these." (Mark 12: 30-31)

The heart and soul are foundational, but as the foregoing verses point out, the connection to, and use of, our mind (our thinking) is also inherently critical to making wise decisions.

Chapter 3 Self-Assessment:
Making Wise Decisions: Heart Matters

Reflections:

1. As you consider business and career decisions do you:
    a. Have a heart-felt reverence for God?
    b. Make prayer a regular part of your daily activity?
    c. Pray regularly about business and career matters?
    d. Seek to find Biblical principles from the Bible?
    e. Memorize scripture to help guide you?
    f. Seek to obey God's preferred way of how you live?
2. Can you think of a time you made a business decision without praying or considering how God might have you view this matter?

Action Steps:

1. If you answered "yes" to question # 2 above, what did you learn from such experiences? Write down the answers.
2. Commit to praying for those for whom you are responsible as well as those in authority over you and start now.
3. What critical business or career matter is weighing on your mind at the moment? Have you prayed and studied the Bible for guidance on this matter? If not, do so now. If you are

doing so, then make the best decision you can based on the facts—leave the rest to God!

4. Name six blessings you can be thankful for right now, with half being business related and half non-business.

Key Bible Verse: Read Jesus's prayer for His management team (His Disciples), John 17: 6-19.

Chapter 3: Footnotes

1. Laurie Beth Jones, *Jesus, CEO,* (New York: Hyperion, 1995), p. 231.
2. Stephen M. McLean, "Lincoln and a Wartime Thanksgiving," *The Wall Street Journal,* (November 26, 2014), p. A-15.

Larry Scanlan

Chapter 4
Making Wise Decisions: Mind Matters

A few weeks into a new job as a mid-level manager in a hospital outside of Philadelphia, my boss Tom (not his real name), called me into his office. I had six supervisors reporting to me in my role as business office manager. He asked me to fire two of them. I asked Tom why he wanted these specific people fired and he curtly commented they were incompetent trouble makers. I prayed, asked the Lord for discernment and formulated a response quickly in my mind.

But first some context is important, because part of what goes into making wise decisions is learning from prior decisions and their consequences. In a previous job at another hospital I had made one of the biggest mistakes of my career in my very first middle management position. The CEO of the organization directed me to fire an admissions office supervisor because several doctors were upset about her performance. So I terminated her as directed. I felt sick over it. In my heart I did not think the physicians who caused this stir had pure motives in their demand; however, I carried out a directive though I felt it wrong. I knew I made a terrible mistake not fighting for the employee. I asked the Lord's forgiveness and promised I would never allow another employee dismissal absent sufficient facts.

Here a couple of years later I was facing a similar scenario with Tom's mandate. After I silently prayed I thought to myself, "here we go Lord" as I said to my boss, "I will not fire them."

I immediately provided him an alternative solution, given I was new to my role and hardly knew my supervisors. I asked him to give me six months to judge the performance of all of my six direct reports and discuss this matter at that time. He reluctantly went along and told me he put the meeting on his calendar.

Almost six months to the day he called me into his office and asked me when I was going to act on the trouble makers. I then explained the two people he wanted fired were my two best supervisors! I thought he would fall off his chair. I presented my case for their performance assessments, sensitively explained the two targeted supervisors were not "yes" people, but that this did not equate to rebellion or incompetence. After a long and tense discussion, the merits and wisdom of each case prevailed. Both supervisors went on to have long careers at the hospital, outlasting both my boss and myself.

Spiritual self-reflection, or "heart matters," is one critical component of making wise decisions; but in addition we must examine the reality of the circumstances upon which we are contemplating a decision. The context of one's reality speaks to head or mind matters.

Knowledge: Seeking facts while avoiding a rush to judgment

We need to obtain the facts of any given situation. But our search for truth comes from a heart desiring to be obedient to God. After all, we want our decisions to make a difference that matters and honors God.

Our decisions have consequences which impact people and organizations. Discernment requires a search for knowledge and truth. A restraint from impulsiveness allows us to ascertain the best course of action, or even non-action. In the age of social media we need to guard against impulsive decisions.

Take for example what happened with the Samsung Galaxy Note 7 smartphone in the fall of 2016. After a number of reports of phones catching on fire the company was under pressure from consumers and telecom operators to act quickly. The company decided the cause was batteries supplied by their own company affiliate and recalled 2.5 million phones. They swapped recalled phones for those supplied by another company.

This decision in September 2016 "to push a sweeping recall based on what turned out to be incomplete evidence…is now coming back to haunt the company," the *Wall Street Journal* reported. The replacement phones also had safety issues, including causing fires, as the company lacked a conclusive answer to the Note 7 problems. The company was originally getting praise from the media for "acting swiftly" in its original recall only to become embarrassed to learn it made a knee jerk decision to quiet the public noise.[1] After taking the time to gather the facts, in January 2017 Samsung announced that both battery companies had problems though they were different kinds of issues. These problems and its ensuing sweeping recall cost the company $5 billion.[2]

Restraint and patience in seeking truth to make decisions may seem slow and annoying to some people, and are, perhaps, even viewed as a lack of decisiveness. Restraint may at times cost us opportunities. Impulsiveness, however, rarely makes good long-term strategic or operational sense, be it for a component of a business or an entire enterprise. Impulsiveness is almost always career limiting.

Determining reality: Fact or fiction?

I was flying one night across the country and had been moved up into first class due to my status as a frequent flyer on a particular airline. However, even sitting in first class, "service" is not exactly something most airlines are known for anymore, regardless of the class of seating. For those who fly, you know if you get good service because it stands out, it is that unusual.

Business Practices, Biblical Promises

On this particular evening, I was sitting in bulkhead on the window side with my computer open, working. I realized at some point the attention and service I was receiving was like nothing I had ever experienced. In addition to the roasted chicken dinner there was the offer of more food from the snack tray along with several offers of various desserts. It seemed like every time I took a sip or two from my drink, the flight attendant came over and leaned over the guy next to me to fill it up again. I thought *wow, what a flight crew, one doesn't usually see this kind of service.* About three-fourths of the way through the flight I noticed this buzz of conversation by four flight attendants at the front of the cabin. One of the flight attendants approached, leaned over to me and said, "you are the Governor of Utah, aren't you, sir?" I, of course, said I was not. That was the last I saw of the "service" for the rest of the flight!

As fate would have it, the very next day, after a series of morning meetings, I was off again, flying to another city, sitting in bulk head, this time on the aisle side. Not long after the flight reached its cruising altitude, the flight attendant came toward me and kneeled beside me.

I quickly thought to myself, "This is great! I don't care what anyone thinks, today I am going to be the Governor of Utah!" She then whispered into my left ear as I anticipated the inevitable question. She said "Sir" (which, not being addressed as Governor, should have been my first clue), "you have a tear in your pants." I felt my face grow hot with embarrassment. Still, I kept my composure and tried to demonstrate my cool by calmly responding, "well how bad can it possibly be?" She responded, "Sir, the tear starts at the midpoint of your back at the waistline, goes straight down about a foot, if you get my drift, and then angles at forty-five degrees over to your right thigh, then continues straight down the back of your right leg and ends just below the back of your knee." In other words, I had a gaping hole in the back of my suit pants. I was about to pass out from the horror of it all but managed to whisper back to her, "you mean when I got up a few minutes ago to go to the…" She did not even let me finish, she interrupted and whispered back "we *all* really enjoyed it!" Talk about a humbling business trip!

On the first leg of my travel the flight attendants made an assumption and acted upon it as if it were a fact: that I was the Governor of Utah. The attendants could have saved themselves a lot of work at the beginning of the flight if they simply tested their assumption but they did not. It is most helpful in the decision-making process to determine if you are dealing with facts versus fiction.

On my part, I made an assumption about the second flight I knew was fictional (thinking I'd pretend to be the Governor) hoping that it would play out as a "fact" so that I could enjoy this little charade I was hoping to pull off. What I got instead were two lessons duly reinforced: one, lying, even to oneself does not pay off, and two, God indeed has a great sense of humor!

Business Practices, Biblical Promises

These business travel stories might seem like an exaggeration to make a point, but fact is often stranger than fiction, and similar incidents do occur in the business world more often than not. For instance, on numerous occasions I have worked with organizations who budget for revenue growth. However, if you look at the assumptions underlying the presumed growth they sometimes are fiction rather than fact.

In other words, an organization is hoping for revenue growth, but there is little basis of reality for which to build such a case. In the consulting world we call this the "revenue fairy strategy." It's like my assumption of being the Governor, hoping it would play out as if the flight crew thought I was him, thus pretending it was all "real." In business, we sometimes buy time hopeful that a positive result will materialize from "thin air." In such cases our decision-making process lacks the vigorous critique of solid theories based on facts, knowledge or truth, together with an honest assessment of reality. Are decisions you are contemplating making based on fact or fiction? Have you done your due diligence? Are you building a business based on hopes, lies or prefabrications—or the truth?

Understanding: More than knowledge and facts

The use of data is critical in our decision-making process. The question is, what do we do with all of this information, how do we use it? Data and information are important, but we still have to use judgment in our decision-making process. Judgement requires more than knowledge, it requires understanding. As Ed Catmull, the founder of Pixar Animation puts it, "measure what you can, evaluate what you measure, and appreciate that you cannot measure the vast majority of what you do." [3]

I made a sales call on a hospital that was in financial trouble. I met the CEO alone and it was clear he was not thrilled about the idea of hiring a consulting firm; however, my appointment was at the behest of his parent organization who was eager to get the financials turned around and cease the weekly bail out checks propping up this organization.

At one point in this meeting the hospital CEO literally threw me the financial statements as he vehemently proclaimed our consulting firm would be hard pressed to find even a dollar in savings given the stellar job his team had done. As I glanced at the statements I could easily see at least twenty-five million dollars in financial improvements could be gained. It was not that I was necessarily smarter than the CEO. After all he and I were looking at the same financial statements, we had the same information (knowledge). The difference was one of *understanding*. I had the benefit of many years of hospital management experience and by this time had gained years of consulting experience with numerous hospitals and health systems throughout the country.

We won the job and our firm identified forty million dollars could be saved in revenue improvements and expense reductions. The CEO was so furious at our findings he did not accept our report. He hired another firm. They found that thirty-six million could be saved. Take either number—both are a far cry from a dollar—and proved the CEO's adamant proclamation that his team had operated as efficiently as possible to be a falsehood. Wise decisions require knowledge *and* understanding.

As we contemplate making decisions, sometimes our evaluation of facts and information generates fear for self-preservation of our jobs and careers and holds us back from facing the reality or truth of our business challenges.[4] Sometimes that fear leads us to manipulate assumptions or twist data to fit a more comfortable scenario or desired state. When honesty is compromised, trust is or will eventually be broken and our business will find itself in jeopardy, along with our job. It takes time to rebuild trust, perhaps a long time. Sometimes it can never be rebuilt. Self-preservation, dysfunctional corporate cultures, and political ideology can distort the seeking and interpreting of facts, impacting the decisions we make. Seeking facts should be a mission to seek understanding. Wise decisions are based on truth.

We should value those around us who speak the truth. "Kings" (leaders) "take pleasure in honest lips; they value the one who speaks what is right." (Proverbs 16: 13)

Seek Advice from Others.

Two CEOs put together one of the largest mergers consummated by two nationally known healthcare organizations at that time. I deeply respected the two executives who led the merger; both had excellent reputations in the industry. After the first year post-merger, they celebrated the "success" of the newly combined hospital enterprise; however, not long thereafter, emerging operating and marketing trends compromised the financial well-being of the combined organization.

Our consulting company was called upon to financially turn around one of the two founding organizations since most of its former senior management was no longer in place. After we gained some traction on the turn-around I worked up the nerve to ask the CEO of the merged hospitals a question. I knew him well enough that I was confident he would be honest in his reply.

I mentioned to him that I was well aware that in putting together this seemingly foresighted merger he had a number of consulting firms and financial advisors (who were paid a lot of money). I said to him, "you have now called upon our firm to fix what has become a broken merger, so why did you not consider our firm's assistance when you were contemplating and planning the merger in the first place?"

I thought he would be honest...and was he ever! "If I had called in your firm and your people thought this merger was not a good idea, I knew you would tell me that," he said.; "And frankly, I did not want anyone saying anything negative about this strategic initiative—I was married to this strategy and I was not about to have anyone suggest this might not be a good idea!"

I was stunned. I knew he was honest, but wow, he had just admitted his decision-making process was not the best way to make such a monumental decision. And monumental it was—the merger was broken up, resulting in a very expensive "fix."

Self-reliance isn't heroic—it's limiting.

It may seem strange that an executive would go about planning a major merger with a mindset of surrounding himself with "yes" advisors. But he is not alone. It happens every day.

I once took an informal poll and asked about a dozen executives if they would be better served by hiring consulting firms who would be truly objective in rendering advice rather than relying on their own knowledge to make decisions. Incredibly, most executives said they wanted consultants who would support their world view; objectivity was not a necessary requirement. Unfortunately, many advisors try to figure out what the boss or client want to hear and feed that message back in hopes of either preserving their own job security or winning more work.

My consulting company was one of two firms that made the final cut in a bid for a performance improvement job for a Kansas hospital. We lost. I called the prospective client's chief financial officer who was spearheading the project and attempted to learn why we lost the job so perhaps we could do better in the future.

One question I asked happened to hit on the salient reason behind this hospital's decision. I asked, "how did our references check out?" There was silence on the other end of the phone for what seemed like a long time. The CFO said our references were fine. I sensed something awry and asked him how our references compared to those of the firm that won, and what differentiated us from our competition? More silence followed. Then he said, "they had no references." I could hardly believe what I had just heard. He then admitted the senior leaders who made the selection wanted an advisory firm they knew they could control, and thus hired a brand new consulting firm that had no track record...no experience. The management team's control (self-reliance) over the "advice" they were presumptively seeking was their paramount agenda.

Self-reliance can lead us to trouble. Are we seeking advice or simply looking to confirm our view? Our effectiveness as formal or informal leaders in our decision-making is reflective of the people with whom we surround ourselves, be it those who are inside or outside the company. "Plans fail for lack of counsel, but with many advisors they succeed." (Proverbs 15:22)

Blind spots

In the Apostle Paul's letter to Timothy, he sounds a warning about surrounding oneself with "a great number of teachers" (advisors), "to say what their itching ears want to hear" and thus "turn their ears away from the truth." (II Timothy 4: 3, 4) All of us have blind spots which can compromise our decision making, or cause the outright failure of our leadership, perhaps damaging our organization. They are called blind spots because we are not aware of our own vulnerability or weaknesses in certain areas. Pointing out our blind spots and assisting us to mitigate them requires reliance upon people who will tell us the truth. It's best to have trusted advisors both inside and outside of your company or circle of influence.

Blinded leaders lack recognition or understanding of the consequences of their decisions according to the authors of the article *Managerial Ethics in Healthcare*, who point to two forms of leadership blindness. The first are those situations in which leaders have incomplete or flawed information upon which their decisions are being made. The second are those in which their deeply held assumptions and beliefs that frame their understanding of their organization and industry influence their behavior and decision making. In essence, it's the lens through which we view the business environment and take actions affecting our organization.[5]

If we believe something to be true when in fact it is not, acting upon our initial false belief is likely to make us feel better in justifying an action or lack of action on our part. Leaders who in essence mislead others lie to themselves first.[6] I am not the Governor of Utah even if I could convince others I am.

Leaders need trusted advisors to help them see what they themselves cannot see. But we must first be willing to be open to the possibility that we have vulnerabilities—we all do. Blind spots that remain will in fact impact the decisions we make along with the consequences we or our organizations experience.

A man of great talent and strength, the Biblical character Samson had two blind spots. One was his need for revenge against people who personally offended or crossed him. Most of us can likely think of leaders like this. The other was his uncontrolled sensuality. We all know people who fit this description given the widespread reporting in 2017-18 of sexual harassment cases by numerous public figures. The consequences of Samson's two blinds spots precipitated his downfall and the loss of his leadership position. (Judges Chapters 15-16) He went from being the Judge of Israel to finishing his life as a prisoner.

As leaders, we may be successful in our own eyes and even in the eyes of others; however, the ability to sustain wise decision making in the long run will depend on our willingness to surround ourselves with people who can help us identify and deal with our blind spots. We may think we are doing the right thing, but we need trusted advisors to hold us accountable from self-centered thinking. As Tim Irwin, PhD, organizational psychologist, management consultant and author, says, "we judge ourselves by our intentions, while others judge us by our behavior." [7]

To reinforce this point of intentions versus behavior, I once worked with a man who was exceptionally brilliant. I admired both his intellect and his great oratorical abilities. He knew he was brilliant and many told him he was. His blind spot was pride. Given his intellectual gifts he felt at times he could make his own rules. *After all,* he thought, *it's about results, right? What does it matter how we get there as long as the results are for the greater good? Doesn't the end justify the means?*

In his last role as the chief executive of a healthcare system he decided certain state regulations were an annoyance, getting in the way of the good things he perceived he was doing. He took some regulatory short-cuts to get a construction project approved. He expected others to go along since, in his mind, this development project was for the greater good. His management team rarely crossed his demeaning, dictatorial management style.

Well into the process he ended up getting caught by state officials. The cost for his blind spot of pride was steep. He not only lost his job but brought much unfavorable publicity to his organization. He served two years in prison and is no longer working in the healthcare industry. As the Bible warns "woe to those who are wise in their own eyes and clever in their own sight." (Isaiah 5:21)

We need to surround ourselves and actively engage with people who will provide us honest feedback. As a leader, appreciate that such advisors often put their own careers and reputation at risk in attempting to help you and your organization. I know, I've been that advisor. But beware of those internal and external advisors who "tickle your ears" or tell you what you want to hear.

Timing

A popular rock song in the 1960's sung by the group The Byrd's entitled "Turn, Turn, Turn," was composed from verses lifted directly from the Bible (Ecclesiastes 3: 1-8).

"There is a time for everything, and a season for every activity under the heavens:
A time to be born and a time to die, a time to plant and a time to uproot,
A time to kill and a time to heal, a time to tear down and a time to build,

A time to weep and a time to laugh, a time to mourn and a time to dance,
A time to scatter stones and a time to gather them, a time to embrace and a time to refrain from embracing,
A time to search and a time to give up, a time to keep and a time to throw away,
A time to tear and a time to mend, a time to be silent and a time to speak,
A time to love and at time to hate, a time for war and a time for peace."

God speaks directly to us about the importance of timing through these verses. Timing impacts our decision making, and thus our ability to execute a plan. In the early 1980's as a young CEO, I made a proposal to my medical staff leadership that our hospital ban patients and employees from smoking. Very few hospitals had such a policy back then. My proposal wasn't because I was smarter or ahead of my time; it was driven by the tragic reality of a patient in a competing hospital who died in a fire from smoking in bed. Smoking seemed like a bad idea for any healthcare enterprise.

I wasn't ten minutes into my little motivational talk to the medical leadership when I looked up and saw that every doctor around the table had lit up a cigarette! The message to me was quite clear; if you move ahead with this proposal we'll send patients to another hospital. Timing was not on my side. Today one would be hard pressed to find hospitals that allow smoking anywhere in their facilities. Timing!

Whether you manage a unit, department, division or entire enterprise, you have or will likely experience an idea, plan or venture you would like to implement. Your passion is deep, and you believe your idea will positively impact your intended customer base. But as you proceed with your decision-making process you experience frustration, wholly or in part because the timing is not lining up. Timing is often out of our control, but it's never out of God's control.

What we call coincidence or providence often has God's invisible hand in "our" plans. Again, we need the discernment, and I would add, patience, to assess if our timing is right in taking or postponing action—in short, in line with God's timing.

King David made extensive plans and preparations for the building of the Temple. (1 Chronicles 22: 5) He had a great vision and did his homework, and had his plans all laid out. However, the Lord had different timing in mind than David did, and thus chose a different leader to build the temple—David's son, Solomon, who would get the responsibility and the limelight for executing what David had initially planned. (1 Chronicles 22: 2-19)

Have you ever planned something where someone else got the recognition or credit? That can be a painful experience and one in which we need God's grace and discernment to understand the greater good in such circumstances. David showed incredible grace and asked God to give his son "discretion and understanding" in his leadership. (1 Chronicles 22:12) We should all pray we will be as gracious as David in similar circumstances God may bring into our career paths.

Being sensitive to timing does test our patience and challenges our rationale. But delay can give us time to gather additional facts, listen to others, refine our plans and allow us to consider if our information correlates with the best timing to take advantage of opportunities and implement those plans. Importantly, it exposes our motive. Are we serving or being self-serving? Is it best for our customers or is it really best for us? How much do we care about the people who will be impacted or affected by the decision? Who benefits more, others or us? Does the intended timing honor God? Remember, "There is a time for everything and a season for every activity under the heavens." (Ecclesiastes 3:1)

Opposition

Opposition doesn't always mean our decision or timing is not right. We need the discernment to know if it is time to move on, or time to stay.

A man owned a successful candy business called Lancaster Caramel. He had bigger dreams to open up a different kind of business within the same industry. But he tired of the harassment of the local politicians' looking to take advantage of him. When he refused to give them "contributions" they increased his property taxes. Rather than fight an uphill battle which would only consume his resources and energy, he moved to a different market, twenty-nine miles northwest. He built a business we know today as Hershey Chocolates.[8] The politicians, impulsively thinking of the moment and of course, themselves, lost a business that today sells products worldwide, employs thousands, and is visited by tourists from all over the world.

Business Practices, Biblical Promises

Milton Hershey decided to move on; however, there are other times when opposition indicates it's time to take a stand. The apostle Paul, in his second missionary journey, faced considerable opposition in Corinth, then a great commercial center of the Roman Empire. (Acts 18:6) The easiest decision would have been to leave and go someplace else. But Paul discerned this was the place where he belonged, and he stayed in Corinth for a year and a half. (Acts 18:11) His decision to stay commenced his ministry to non-Jews, a change from his previous focus. Taking a stand in the face of opposition brought the gospel to a whole lot more people.

Our firm once faced opposition from a CEO who was displeased with our advice on cutting costs. He demanded further cuts than we recommended. We believed going beyond our recommendations would compromise patient care, so we refused. We resigned from the job. More consulting fees weren't worth jeopardizing our reputation or our client's well-being. Sometimes opposition tests your resolve and the principles upon which you conduct business.

Act: make a decision.

Wise decisions are a matter of both the heart and mind. The heart speaks to our internal view of God: our reverence of Him, our dialogue (prayer) with Him, and our desire to truly follow and be obedient to Him, all enhanced by knowledge of His word, the Bible. Our mind assesses external circumstances. There is usually plenty of information and data available for most situations, and at times perhaps too much. Becoming familiar with Biblical principles as we study data and facts is imperative to making wise decisions. We filter information within God's guardrail, the Bible, in the context of our training, workplace and life experiences.

I for one have never heard an audible voice from God that led me to a decision. I think many people can resonate with this. Perhaps you look for "signs" from God. But in my experience, I believe that God rarely reveals the future to us when we are contemplating business or personal decisions. Our faith and our efforts to seek the truth would be compromised by knowing the future for our own selfish reasons. God's will is not a dot in the sky; it is a field of opportunity within God's guardrails as presented in the Bible.

So as I seek to move from knowledge to understanding when making decisions or taking action, I pray, study the Bible, research the facts, evaluate the circumstances (reality) and ask others for advice. I also evaluate timing and assess opposition and risk. As I contemplate decisions through a Biblical lens, my motives become clearer. His Word is powerful and thus it is able to confirm my obedience (or convict my lack thereof).

For example, I, along with some other partners, bought our consulting company from its founders in 1998 which meant taking on debt, resulting in considerable business risk. I had to examine my decision in the context of what the Bible says about debt, which is frankly plenty. I also went to God's Word to learn more about alliances because I was going to be working with a number of partners. The Bible warns us about being bound together with unbelievers, and challenges us to examine such partnerships in the context of commonality versus conflict. (2 Corinthians 6: 14-16)

This deeper understanding led us to negotiate bank terms enabling us to buy the business without jeopardizing our personal assets. Absent such terms, I would have walked away. Today such terms would not even be possible given changes in bank regulations, so timing was on our side. Information (data and facts) was critical, but what made the process clearer in terms of making a wise decision was my search for Biblical principles on the issues of debt and business partnerships (alliances), and timing. Knowledge should lead to understanding. Understanding is enhanced when applied against the filter of God's Word, giving us wisdom to act or restrain from action.

God blessed our talented company. In leading our firm as its President, my partners and I were privileged and humbled to double the size of the company in four years. Our success and national reputation positioned us to receive offers to buy our company. We sold the company in 2002 for a sufficient return on our investment. We then helped lead our new owner, Navigant consulting, a publicly traded company, build its hospital provider practice.

In summary, having done the homework of both the heart and mind, we make our wisest decisions in a spirit of humility and leave the rest to God. Our faith and security are ultimately in Him, not our position, title or paycheck. Our relationship with Him is forever, our job and our leadership roles are training for eternity. The outward result may or may not end up how we preferred it or even pictured it in our limited view; however, God knows our heart and the work that goes into making our decisions. Do your homework, decide, then rest in Him, trust in Him. (Proverbs 3:5,6)

Chapter 4 Self-Assessment:
Making Wise Decisions: Mind Matters

Reflections:

1. Can you think of an impulsive decision you wish you could take back?
2. Have you ever had an idea that someone else implemented and/or got credit for?
3. Have you gotten credit for an idea largely the work of someone else?
4. If so, have you thanked them or given them recognition?
5. Do you find your search for truth taking a back seat to political correctness or your company's corporate culture?

Action Steps:

1. As it pertains to your current business responsibilities, what key business assumptions underpin your operations and decisions? As you think further about those assumptions, if those assumptions are *not* correct what are the implications for your business? Your career? Write down the answers.

2. What's the most pressing business issue facing you at this moment that is time critical?

a. Are you certain it is time critical? If so set deadlines.

b. What likely will happen if you miss the anticipated time line? Make sure you have a schedule in place to meet your deadlines.

3. Determine if the advice you receive this coming week is best for your organization or if it constitutes advice people believe you want to hear!

4. Ask your most trusted advisors to name your blind spot(s).

a. Then ask your spouse or significant other.

b. What will you do about these and when? Write down your answers.

5. Thank those people who risk giving you advice they believe is truly best for you and your organization.

Key Bible Verses: Read and contemplate Ecclesiastes 3: 1-8; John 7:1-8; Proverbs chapters 4 and 8. Also Proverbs 3:21-23; 15:22; 20:18; 23:19.

Chapter 4: Footnotes

1. Jonathan Cheng and John D. McKinnon, "Samsung Recalls's Fatal Flaw," *The Wall Street Journal* (October 24, 2016)., pp. A1, A12.

2. Timothy W. Martin and John D. McKinnon, "Samsung Traces Battery Problem," *The Wall Street Journal* (January 21-22, 2-17), p. B1.
3. Ed Catmull, *Creativity, Inc.* (New York: Random House, 2014), pp. 219-220.
4. Ibid., p. 85
5. William A. Nelson, PhD, HFACHE, "Avoiding Blinded Healthcare Leadership," *Healthcare Executive* (November-December 2014), p. 46.
6. Tim Irwin, PhD, *Impact: Great Leadership Changes Everything* (Dallas, TXL BenBella Books, 2014), p. 113.
7. Ibid., p. 42.
8. Michael D'Antonio, *Hershey* (New York: Simon & Schuster, 2006), pp. 99-101.

Larry Scanlan

Part II

Our Plan Will Carry the Day… *Or Will It?*

Larry Scanlan

Chapter 5

Vision and Mission: *Where* Are We Going and *Why?*

"Where there is no vision, the people perish" (Proverbs 31:18).[1]

A company's purpose is often described in a vision statement defining the reason for the business. It addresses *where* the business is heading, or its desired future state. In other words, the vision speaks to the overarching objective of the enterprise.

When George H. Bush was President of the United States he admitted several times he never got the "vision thing," as he called it, which his predecessor, Ronald Reagan, so effectively communicated to the country. It's one reason Mr. Bush was a one-term President. President Reagan conveyed his belief that our spiritual commitment would win the struggle for peace far more so than our military power, as God in His providence would bless such a commitment. It is no small miracle that American hostages held in Iran for over a year were released on Ronald Reagan's first day in office in January 1981—without a shot being fired. Nor was it coincidental that the cold war effectively ended through his negotiation and his professional relationship with his Russian counterpart conducted over his two terms in office.

Vision: *Where* we aim must be achievable, believable, and credible.

A clearly articulated vision engenders buy-in from a company's workers and produces a strong sense of meaning and direction. Visions must be embraced.

A headline in the *Wall Street Journal* six months after the company went public in 2014 read "Twitter CEO Struggles to Define Vision." The article described a meeting during which the CEO called in his management team and drew three circles on the board. One circle represented social media users, a second depicted visitors to the Twitter site, and the third circle represented Twitter content on other websites. He instructed his staff that this was the new way to target markets going forward as opposed to just focusing on Twitter's active users. His management team was bewildered. It was the first time the team had heard of this change of direction, prompted by competitive pressures. Twitter employees described this experience as reflective of the CEO's management style of bouncing from one idea to the next, being a reactive thinker.

The scrutiny of running a public company left the CEO struggling to convey a consistent vision for the business, resulting in personnel changes and defections.[2] Roll forward two years to 2016—Twitter's lackluster user and revenue growth rate caused the company to consider a sale.[3] In the spring of 2017, given the lack of a sale, Twitter announced its co-founder was returning to the company to focus on its culture "in an attempt to revive morale amid many executive departures and slumping growth."[4] The company has stabilized and in 2018 reported its first ever quarterly profits.

Companies indeed struggle when their vision is not clear or consistent. We know from the Bible a series of judges ruled over Israel for about 200 years, beginning around 1375 BC. The next to last Old Testament judge was a man named Eli. He, perhaps like our Twitter CEO described above, reacted to situations rather than laying out a clear vision and taking decisive action. Eli' was more concerned with symbolism than substance. He viewed the Ark of the Covenant more a relic (symbol) to be protected instead of putting his focus on the Protector, God. It seems some people in our day view God and church as old-fashioned "relics" not relevant to daily business and life. Well, Eli's judgeship ended in failure (I Samuel 1-4), as the ark was captured by Israel's enemies in Eli's last military battle. Today local churches that have lost their vision have had their places of worship converted to other uses or are simply sitting empty.

Most of us have likely worked with or observed leaders focused more on symbolism rather than a substantive vision. They don't walk the talk. Perhaps a memorable vision of symbolism over substance was the United Airline customer who was dragged off of the airplane to "rectify" an overbooking situation in the spring of 2017. This from an airline whose motto was "the friendly skies." That image reminded me of the airline attendant I once encountered who told those of us within hearing distance we'd understand what customer service is when we realize we are treated just like checked-in luggage! That put airline travel into a new perspective for me.

In September of 2016 the CEO of Lands' End, Inc., the fashion retailer, was forced to resign after only nineteen months on the job. During her brief tenure Federica Marchionni's vision was to bring more style to this maker of outdoor casual clothes. She attempted to add different styles to their clothing line, revamped the catalog and hired celebrity photographers. Despite her efforts, the employees never bought into this vision. Furthermore, she worked most times out of an office in New York rather than in the company's headquarters in Dodgeville, Wisconsin, an additional point of angst with employees.[5] The optics and substance of our actions must be consistent with our vision if we hope to retain a committed team or workforce.

A leader may possess great zeal and be closely identified with the vision of his or her organization. But zeal doesn't always effectively carry out a company's vision. A study conducted of 16,000 people who started companies found that *passion* best described such entrepreneurs. Though passion is a positive, it can also be a negative, the study said, because "passionate entrepreneurs are so impatient to move forward with their brilliant new idea that they get too optimistic about how would-be customers and investors will see it. They don't realize the skills and support they need to get a business on its feet."[6]

Business Practices, Biblical Promises

Obtaining the necessary sales, technical and management experience takes an investment of time and money that cannot be covered purely through passion. I have seen my share of entrepreneurs, established business executives and religious leaders who articulate their vision with high energy and passionate zeal, but who have little accomplishment to show for it. Visions require more than an idea with an over-abundance of enthusiasm or emotion. Vision statements must meet the "ABC"s: they must be achievable, believable and credible.

Mission: *What* **we do to achieve our vision**

The mission statement articulates *what* will be done to achieve the vision; it speaks to the present.

Several years ago, I was having my windshield replaced at an auto repair shop in Clearwater, Florida. Upon completion, the gentleman who repaired it asked me how I liked the car; it was about six years old at the time. I told him I really enjoyed the way it rode and how reliable the car had been for me. I inquired as to why he asked, and he replied the particular year and model of my 2005 Lexus was considered the closest the company had come to perfection in making a car. (I kept it for twelve years, 286,000 miles). I immediately thought of the Lexus motto, "in pursuit of excellence."

Consider these mission statements from company websites:

Lexus: "We are an automotive company that takes inspired design, relentless innovation and uninhibited performance and turns them into passionate, moving experiences."

D.R. Horton, describing the vision of its founder of more than 35 years ago: "Of livable and affordable new homes built with unmatched efficiencies and uncompromising quality. Of family tradition passed on to new generations. Of a business that would grow by making customers' dreams a reality."

Peirce College (Philadelphia, PA): "We empower adult learners to improve their lives by achieving career goals through academic offerings aligned with evolving workforce needs."

University of Maryland Upper Chesapeake Health (Harford County, MD): "We deliver an exceptional care experience for every person, every encounter, every day."

What constitutes a sustainable mission?

I always resonated with famous management consultant and author Peter Drucker's advice on missions. Known as the "founder of modern management," Drucker's view is that successful and sustainable missions possess three equally important components:[7]

Competence: What is it we do well? Many organizations aim to grow and sometimes get into diverse lines of business, but of which knowledge and skills are we truly masters? When Drucker wrote his book on non-profit organizations he cited hospitals as examples of organizations that do *not* do prevention very well. Today as this book is written, hospitals and doctors are taking on the role of financial risk for outcomes of care, like an insurance company, given the "incentives" of wellness and prevention as mandated by the Affordable Care Act. Time will tell if an insurance-like mentality really fits the sweet spot of caring for the sick, let alone makes hospitals, doctors and nurses masters of "prevention."

For-profit companies face the same challenge. Campbell Soup's CEO was forced to resign in May of 2018. As consumer taste changed, the company acquired businesses to better position it in the fresh food business. But the focus on these businesses proved to be outside the core competence of the company. Soups sales, the core of its business, fell in six of the seven years of the CEO's tenure resulting in her resignation.[8]

What is it your company really does well? What do you do well?

Commitment: What do we really truly believe and embrace? Is the mission we or our organizations profess lived out by employees and team members? A survey of over thirty-six thousand employees determined that one in eight cited their employer's mission as the main reason they stay on the job.[9]

What happens when a company strays from its mission? Facebook for example has experienced the defection of employees who saw its privacy practices at odds with the mission for which they originally joined the company. Sometimes dissenters' voices are unfortunately lost in such circumstances when "group think" dominates and dictates politically correct or economically driven workplace business practices.[10]

What are we truly committed to doing? One consulting firm of which I was in charge was not very good at supply chain consulting. Supplies usually comprised about fifteen to twenty percent of a hospital's controllable cost, but we never could bring ourselves to invest in the talent required to do that work because it was not our sweet spot. Rather we committed our skills to the larger opportunities found in either labor expense or revenue interventions, thus we sub-contracted for the residual supply-chain expertise. No one or no one organization can be good at everything. And whatever your unit, department or organization is good at doing, it likely will do it considerably better if your people are truly committed to it.

Opportunities: In a world where the internet and technology have created a multitude of disruptive enterprises (competitors), your business is going to change, thus leaving room for new opportunities. Opportunities speak to addition—and subtraction. New opportunities raise the issue of "organizational fit." Can you truly make the commitment of resources and talent required to achieve the desired outcome or results? I find most organizations, especially non-profits, become readily enthused about adding services but reticent about closing or exiting a line of service. Sometimes a business needs to subtract or close services so that it can leave room for new opportunities. Sometimes a service is no longer a good fit and you have to just say "no."

Challenge the mission's relevance.

Management and the board of directors or trustees should re-assess their organization's mission statement annually. If you are the leader of a component of your business, be it a unit, department, division or squad, your job is to define the mission for your sphere of responsibilities within the broader vision of your company. Before commencing annual budget cycles, critique your mission for relevance.

If a service or product does not make good customer sense or good business sense, it is time to call that portion of the mission over.

For example, in the past, some hospitals were formed primarily to serve religious or racial minorities, particularly those of Jewish faith and African Americans. This pertained not only to patients but to doctors who often were barred from obtaining privileges to practice at other hospitals. I was the project director for my consulting firm when one of our clients, the last African American hospital in Baltimore (Provident, later named Liberty), merged with a Catholic hospital. Fortunately, the level of discrimination that had fostered the original vision and mission for such hospitals had changed for the better after many years of struggle for racial and religious equality, therefore resulting in the need to refocus the merged hospital's mission.

There are other organizations where the missions were substantially fulfilled. Specialty facilities such as tuberculosis treatment centers are no longer around—mission accomplished. The March of Dimes once focused on polio. When this disease was virtually eradicated in the United States, the organization had the foresight to change its vision and today its mission is to focus on birth defects.

Absent foresight, changes can blindside the mission of an enterprise. In the 1990's Blockbuster Video had thousands of stores across the country and other parts of the world. It missed the changes in technology and delivery as competitors (Redbox, Netflix, On Demand to name a few) formed to take market share. Blockbuster was forced to file for bankruptcy. One would be hard pressed to find a Blockbuster store today.

As a personal example, in my family's genealogy I had several generations of relatives who were blacksmiths. Originally from Ireland, they later immigrated and performed the same work in Philadelphia, PA. However, modes of transportation eventually changed, and their business and skill set were no longer applicable for their community's greater benefit. Each of us must assess if our skills are relevant, marketable or transferrable.

Business Practices, Biblical Promises

I am familiar with a faith-based school that provides formal education as well as after-hours programs to school age kids in Camden, New Jersey, one of the most impoverished and dangerous cities in the United States. This school, Urban Promise, resides in a part of the city that doesn't even have a library. For years, the school needed more space and eventually purchased a former church building across the street. How the church became available for purchase is quite a story, and a lesson to contemplate applicable to both vision and mission.

Given its location, the church was struggling to grow. During one particular service, the minister decided to have a discussion with the congregation on what needed to be done to make their neighborhood safer and a more vibrant area in which to live, work and worship. The congregation came up with ten issues needing action. The minister then set up ten stools in front of the sanctuary and put a clipboard with a sheet of paper on each one. He then challenged the congregation to come up front and take ownership by signing on to help work toward solutions for one of these ten areas.

He waited for a few minutes, and then waited some more. No one, not one person, signed up to take ownership for any of the very needs they themselves identified as necessary for their community. The community needs were obvious, but if you don't have followers to help carry out the work, then you have nothing for which to lead. Furthermore, commitment calls for more than followers with brains—you need their hearts and bodies to do the work. This church had a mission for sure, it had *opportunity* and it perhaps had *competence* within the membership, but the entire membership lacked *commitment*.

The next day the minister called a meeting of his board and stated there was no future for this church. The leaders agreed and decided to close the church and sell the building, which is how the school eventually ended up with a much-needed extra space for its classrooms. The school had a mission supported by competence, opportunity and commitment—the church did not. The school is still relevant, the church is gone.

Is your organization or company still relevant? If it went out of business would customers truly miss it or be disadvantaged? At times the mission of a business or a line of business is no longer relevant and the vision needs to be redirected or perhaps even declared complete. That is a very tough call for most leaders, but one sometimes required.

What is *your* vision and mission?

Perhaps you are the leader of a unit. Or maybe you lead a squad or platoon in the military; or you lead a department, or division; or perhaps you have an executive role over an entire enterprise. What is the mission for your sphere of influence within your company's broader vision and mission? How does your vision and mission impact other people?

In the Old Testament book of Daniel, King Nebuchadnezzar

admired the work he accomplished to carry out his vision of building an empire no matter what it cost other people. It was all about him, and it eventually came back to haunt him.   He so admired his own accomplishments and greatness that God decided to teach him a lesson. God had him suddenly removed from leadership and he lost his "business," his empire. He was "homeless," literally surviving by eating grass. His hair and finger nails grew unwieldy as he was slowly going insane. When he finally acknowledged that God rules the heavens and the earth, including those who sit in leadership, his throne was restored to him. Nebuchadnezzar finally understood "those who walk in pride He is able to humble." (Daniel 4:28-37)

Visions and missions have consequences; they do make a difference. Leaders have accountability for the outcome of missions conducted in the name of a grander vision. Look at what the Bible says in one instance when the vision and mission get off track:

> *"Woe to the sinful nation, a people whose guilt is great, a brood of evildoers, children given to corruption! They have forsaken the Lord; they have spurned the Holy One and turned their backs on him. Your whole head is injured, your whole heart afflicted. From the sole of your foot to the top of your head there is no soundness.   Your country is desolate, your cities burned with fire; your fields are being stripped by foreigners right before you, laid waste as when overthrown by strangers."* (Isaiah 1: 4, 5b, 6a, 7)

This sounds like it was written for our very own time and place, but it was written about 700 BC by the prophet Isaiah in reference to Israel turning its back on God. The mission of one's life or business in opposition to God's principles ultimately carries a great cost.

Contrast this story with the Old Testament character Nehemiah. He had a vision to rebuild the walls of Jerusalem. He put substance to that vision by patrolling and exploring every aspect of the city. He came up with the mission to rebuild the city and a plan to implement it. When he later explained his vision and laid out the mission, the peoples' response was "let us start rebuilding." (Nehemiah 2: 18) The people bought into both the vision and the mission and jumped right into it.

This brings us to perhaps the most important question: what is the vision you have for your life? The vision for your life will impact how you lead and carry out the vision and mission of your company within your sphere of influence and responsibility. Your life vision and philosophy will influence your company's business and its intended purpose; furthermore, you will affect others around you, especially those you are responsible for leading. As Tim Irwin, PhD puts it, "beliefs determine our behavior, both our actions and our emotions." Furthermore, "what a leader believes about those he or she leads plays a dominant role in whether or not the heart and minds of followers are engaged."[11]

It is a matter of life priority and career priority. Is God first in our lives? Review your checkbook, examine the calendar, and peruse the contact list on the smart phone. Then ask your spouse or most trusted friend how they see you addressing this question. You will have an idea who is first in your life. You'll have a clear understanding of the purpose (mission) for which you are living.

In what is known as the "Great Commission," Jesus' final instruction to his disciples was to spread the Gospel, to "go and make disciples of all nations." (Matthew 28:19) This great commission expanded the mission from its previous focus on those of the Jewish faith to now include everyone, the entire world. Before Jesus ascended to heaven He made sure the disciples understood the relevance and scope of their mission.

Are you on a mission that is relevant to making a God honoring difference in your family, community and place of business?

Chapter 5 Self-Assessment:
Vision and Mission: *Where* Are We Going and *Why*?

Reflections:

1. Can you confidently say that the vision for your life is congruent with God's word?
2. Does your company's vision foster you honoring God in your work?
3. Within your sphere of influence do you have a clear mission for your role?
4. If your company went out of business would many customers be adversely affected?

Actions Steps:

1. Within your area of influence in your company, when is the last time you critiqued your vision and mission statement? If it has been a long time, do so now.
2. If you don't have a vision for the unit for which you are responsible, create one which fits within the overall vision of your company.
3. If you do have a mission for your area of influence, is it fresh? Competition, technology and consumer preferences change; thus, is the vision and mission still relevant? If not, write a new one.

Business Practices, Biblical Promises

Key Bible Verses: Read and contemplate Proverbs 29:18; vision and missions need followers: read Matthew 9:35-38.

Chapter 5: Footnotes

1. Frank Charles Thompson, DD., PhD., *The New Chain-Reference Bible* (Indianapolis, Indiana: B.B. Kirkbride Bible Co., Inc., 1964), p. 630

2. Yoree Koh and Kirsten Grind, "Twitter CEO Costolo Struggles to Define Vision," *The Wall Street Journal*, (November 7, 2014), p. B1.

3. Yoree Koh, "Some Lose Faith in Twitter's CEO," *The Wall Street Journal*, (October 6, 2016), p. B1.

4. Georgia Wells, "Twitter Co-Founder Returns to Coop Amid Departures," *The Wall Street Journal*, (May 17, 2017), p. B4.

5. Suzanne Kapner and Joann S. Lublin, "Lands" End CEO Is Pushed Out After 19 Months," *The Wall Street Journal*, (September 27, 2016), p. B1

6. Noam Wasserman, "Zeal Can Destroy a Startup," *The Wall Street Journal*, (August 25, 2014), p. R1.

7. Peter F. Drucker, *Managing The Nonprofit Organization* (New York, NY: HarperCollins Publishers, 1990), p. 7, 8.

8. Aaron Back, "Campbell Soup's Can of Worms." "Sales Woes Force Out Campbell's CEO," *The Wall Street Journal*, (May 19-20, 2018), pp. B12, B1.

9. Sue Shellenbarger, "When Companies Benefit From Naysayers," *The Wall Street Journal,* (September 18, 2018), p. A13.
10. Ibid.
11. Tim Irwin, PhD, *Impact: Great Leadership Changes Everything* (Dallas, TX: BenBella Books, 2014), p. 88,123

Chapter 6

Planning: *How* Will We Accomplish Our Mission?

A man addressing a large crowd asked a rhetorical question about building. It could easily be about building a business or a career. He asked his audience if they were responsible for building something wouldn't they first sit down and estimate the cost to see if there was enough money? Or if they wanted to effectively compete in a line of business would they not make sure they had enough talent to do so? The person to whom I'm referring who was asking these questions and addressing the crowd was Jesus! (Luke 14: 28-32)

I had a hospital client who entered into a new line of business, that of health insurance It's a significantly different business from running hospitals and entails taking substantial financial risk, especially when attempting to take market share away from long established competitors.

When I individually interviewed each member of the client's board of directors, one common concern ran through their responses. To put it in their terms, they wanted to know "how much cash is this new cow going to eat?" In other words, they had approved of entering into a new line of business, but were not informed, nor did they ask management, about the potential total investment required to make this business successful until after it was already underway. After informing the CEO and COO of the collective feedback of the board members, I then asked them if they had an exit strategy in case this new line of business did not work. They candidly looked at me and said they never thought about an exit strategy. They had not fully evaluated the total potential cost of this new investment, as Jesus had counseled about such things over 2,000 years ago!

This chapter is not about the mechanics of planning, but rather, once having gathered sufficient data and information pursuant to the planning process, asking, "what are the principles we use to make wise judgments and decisions based on that data and information." In other words, what are the planning principles that guide us on *how* to fulfill our mission? We'll examine five such principles.

The past: historical context

In the spring of 2016 my wife and I were in Poland, a country which over the last few centuries had been torn apart by the control of foreign countries, particularly Russia and Germany. Our guide lamented his concern about remembering the hard lessons of those years as he mentioned their young people don't spend much time in school studying or understanding his country's history. We responded we have the same concern for our own country.

Jeremiah of the Old Testament raised this very concern and offered his counsel: "stand at the crossroads and look; ask for the ancient paths, ask where the good way is." (Jeremiah 6: 16a) What is meant by the ancient paths? This in part refers to history: what has been your company's history, what have you done before and why? What has worked and what has not gone as planned?

History, the "ancient paths," is an important context in deciding strategic direction or repositioning for the present and future. If your company is new or very young, you are making history which will become a reference point for those who follow you. If your company is well established, its history is one important factor in the deliberations of updating the strategic plan.

This is not to say history is to be an impediment to substantive change in direction; however, to ignore history is to ignore important lessons, both good and bad. To diminish the past is often to the detriment of the future of our business and our careers.

Mr. Joe Lieberman, former U.S. Senator and once a candidate for Vice President of the United States, wrote an article on the history and linkage between two Jewish holidays. Passover, as most know, celebrates the liberation of the Israelites from slavery, while Shavuot commemorates the Giving of the Law to Moses on Mount Sinai, the Ten Commandments. One holiday, Passover, is about freedom, while the other, Shavuot, is about God's gift of law and purpose. One without the other would bring chaos. A society, business or career of only freedom absent a moral compass would not distinguish well between right and wrong.[1] History provides leaders and followers objective lessons on what has been accomplished and what has been missed. Such assessments are important to any strategic planning process.

Jesus himself often talked about history, emphasizing lessons from the past to guide us today. In one conversation Jesus was asked by the Pharisees to perform a miracle to prove who He was. He responded that if they understood the lessons from the Old Testament prophet Jonah, or understood King Solomon's counsel, the questioners would have known who He, Jesus, really was—standing right in front of them. (Matthew 12: 38-42) But the questioner lacked accurate historical context. At times the lessons of history are right in front of us but we don't know it. We need to be sufficiently informed about the past to understand the lessons it has to offer for the present, let alone future implications.

A great story of the consequences of not considering the "ancient ways" and "good paths" is relayed to us in the two Old Testament books, 2 Kings Chapter 22; and 2 Chronicles Chapter 34, which are both applicable to our own current culture today. The Bible, or the Book of the Law as it was known then, was literally pushed out of public life over a period of years, much akin to what has actively taken place in our own society for the last sixty years.

Through a series of godless leaders, the Book of the Law had literally disappeared, and thus became irrelevant to how people conducted their business or personal lives. They had no need to refer to something that was not even around. Then during the reign of King Josiah (about 640 BC), someone found the Book in the Temple. When the king had someone read the scroll to him he was so taken back by the gap between the "ancient ways" and the contemporary culture his despair caused him to literally tare his robe. He was overwhelmed by how evil and political correctness had shoved God's word out of the culture to the point where Biblical principles were absent from the society, including in their business practices. Worshipping idols, practicing witchcraft and even sacrificing children had become imbedded in the culture. The chasm between the "good way" and what was being lived out daily was staggering.

In the development of your strategic plan, be knowledgeable of the history of the enterprise. Be aware your current planning efforts will engender decisions that make their own history which will impact future leaders and workers. Plans, good or bad, have consequences. Good planning at a minimum takes history, or "the ancient ways," into account.

Present and future business opportunities

The desired future of a business is the fulfillment of its vision. Designing a future that will make a difference for our customers requires us to critique what we are currently doing. (Lamentations 3: 40) Test your products or services in three areas: their alignment with your company's historical context as mentioned above; their present state of performance; and their projected future relevance.

One principle of planning is what *not* to do. Don't get caught up with the pride of your own previous or current success. In the Old Testament book of Hosea (chapter 13:6), the Lord admonishes "when I fed them, they were satisfied, when they were satisfied, they became proud; then they forgot me." This describes what sometimes happens in today's business, political, educational and cultural institutions. Pride eventually leads to adverse consequences. Past and current success is no guarantee of future success.

Furthermore, in critiquing our present business model we are instructed to examine and test ourselves to confirm if we are walking the faith we say we believe. (2 Corinthians 13: 5) Is what we do in the work place making sense? If our product, service, or business disappeared would customers truly miss it, or do they have such a variety of choices we would soon be forgotten? Does it make sense to keep doing it? Do our customers want more of it, or less of it?

What about growth opportunities? All businesses want to grow, and we as leaders also need to grow. Where are those opportunities? As data and information is gathered and studied, what opportunities make sense for the future of the business? Do we have the resources of talent, facilities and equipment to do a credible and God-honoring job?

A CEO brought together his leaders and instructed them to go out and examine a new market for his "company" to enter. He asked them to go see it first hand, check out the people, the demographics, the geography, the barriers of entry, its neighborhoods, explore it in as much depth as possible and report back to him. Twelve people, all experienced professionals, comprised this planning task force. They spent six weeks analyzing and observing in detail this potential new market opportunity. When they came back and gave their findings to the CEO and COO, ten of the twelve reported that it would be difficult to take on this new market and they strongly advised against pursuing it. Two however, who examined the same exact information and data as the others, said the opportunity was achievable, they should go for it.

Now think about this planning process. Twelve leaders had access to the same visuals and information but two reported back and gave a different interpretation of the analysis and thus a different recommendation than ten others. This puts a boss in a difficult circumstance; in which direction should he or she proceed? The easy answer would be to think that following the minority report of the two would be a little crazy, given ten others were united in their opposition to pursue this new market.

The foregoing is actually a true historical account from the Old Testament book of Numbers (Chapter 13) in which Moses and Aaron (the CEO and COO respectively) ask twelve advisors to assess the value of taking over the "market" known as Canaan (the Promised Land). To jump ahead, it turned out the minority report was actually correct; however, the other ten were united as to reporting the risks associated with pursuing a breakaway strategy.

Their determination to stick with the status quo, along with their ensuing spread of dissension in the ranks caused the "company" to forfeit any immediate or even short-term ability to acquire the Promised Land. They would wait forty more years before again having an opportunity to reach this "new market." In business, such missed opportunities are often lost forever. Sometimes the minority report is right and the risks are worth taking to reap the vast rewards.

In my consulting experience, I have seen my fair share of strategic plans sitting on a shelf, not being followed. Many such plans were quite good, but were put to the side because the execution of the plan required difficult actions, some of which would offend or upset one or more constituents; therefore, little was done beyond treading water or pursing the path of least resistance.

Looking at this Biblical story of the "planning committee" from a business perspective; their obvious fear and "group think" paralyzed most of the planning task force. The hard work that would be required to conquer a new market was more than they were willing to take on, despite the enormous and obvious advantages. Think about it; all twelve of the leaders came back and agreed unanimously that the market was excellent; however, ten saw the barriers to entry as being too much to overcome. Only two felt a unified, faithful and focused effort would give them successful entry to a new market. Fear can be just as debilitating as satisfaction with the status quo. In business we sometimes forfeit future opportunities given our comfort with the present or fear of the future. We won't achieve our vision without taking intelligent risks.

Is your plan realistic?

Another reason strategic plans collect dust from my experience is that sometimes they are not realistic. "They who chase fantasies have no sense." (Proverbs 12:11b) Probably many of us can relate to stories where plans and budgets seemed, at least in part, based on something other than reality. Is the plan for your area of influence practical?

Our firm was trying to finalize a contract to assist a well-known academic medical center on the east coast. Their plan was off-target, causing considerable financial shortfalls from what had been originally projected, bringing into question the credibility of their assumptions.

There was great consternation among the renowned faculty and medical leaders regarding the need for hiring outside help and especially questioning as to why our particular firm was being hired. Our team was sitting along the walls in the meeting in a large board room, fittingly furnished with one of the largest boardroom tables I had ever seen. The debate taking place right in front of us was so candid it was as if we were not even in the room, but rather like we were flies on the wall! I rarely had ever experienced anything as openly honest, if not hostile, as the tension that filled the room. It was surreal.

The President was at the head of the table and the meeting turned on a question addressed to him, "why do want to hire *these* guys?" I sat against the wall, my heart pounding in anticipation of his answer. He responded, "We're hiring this firm because if there were a dead horse lying on the middle of this board room table, half of us would deny the horse was dead and the other half would want to study it." This firm would tell us the horse is dead!" We got the engagement!

It's important not to be deceived by denial nor be overly in love with our own ideas in judging the reality of our plan and trying to figure out its future marketability. An outside trusted and objective advisor can be especially helpful in critiquing the relevance of your strategic plan to the market place. Why? Because you need someone who is sufficiently experienced and discerning to speak the truth and tell you when "the horse is dead."

In my first career job working for a large accounting firm I remember a senior accountant humorously relaying an experience he encountered. In auditing the inventory of a food store, he found an enormous amount of cherry pies sitting in the inventory and wondered why. Upon investigation, he learned the purchasing director had ordered the cherry pies using the month of February as a proxy. By choosing the one month in which the most cherry pies are sold (think George Washington and the cherry tree) he had overbought and thus significantly overstocked the bakery's need for cherry pies. This was a terrible waste of inventory space and money.

But to some degree we are all guilty of lacking realism in our plans. We all know family and friends who bought houses and even businesses before the Great Recession of 2007. Their credit scores and cash position should have dictated not doing so; however, easy credit, flexible mortgage rates, and assumptions about increasing real estate values caused many to make decisions that in hindsight we now see were unrealistic. The facts were right in front of us when those decisions were made in the first place. It's the same in the strategic planning process of our business unit, or company—plans with their corresponding required actions must be based on reality, not on what we hope will happen. Unrealistic hope usually results in substituting short-term gain for long-term pain.

I was called into an organization which five years previously had made a decision to plan for a new hospital as the cornerstone of their strategic direction. Their key assumption in the previous planning period projected volume trends predicting profits would continue to climb. However, it was painfully clear five years later they were in no position to build a new hospital because they were running out of cash! How did this happen? The assumption that profit trends would continue upward lacked reality. Looking back the organization had reached its peak five years prior and their administrators either did not know that or didn't want to admit it.

Are the current trends of your unit or business truly indicative of the future? Reality requires asking the questions most would rather not ask, along with a rigorous pursuit for practical answers or options.

If you're in the real estate business and selling in a hot market, one needs the discipline in the planning process to regularly put money away for the inevitable downturn in the housing market. A plan that does not take into account a business cycle in such an industry is fantasy planning. That's one reason why in real estate, eighty percent of the commissions are earned by only twenty percent of the realtors (disclosure, I once had a real estate license). It's hard work and requires realistic planning to withstand an inevitable adverse business cycle. Are we planning based on the reality of our industry's future, including its business cycles?

Fire in the belly: Do we really believe in the plan?

In one of my roles in running a nationally known consulting firm, my colleagues would pressure me at times to hire friends who were out of work. Most of these unemployed executives were in their predicament because their former organization was failing and they did not seek or hire the right kind of help. Some would specifically avoid hiring a firm like ours, a turnaround firm who did not take to fools lightly. I refused to hire people whose own pride prevented them from contracting for the right kind of help when they needed it the most.

I had learned from experience these unemployed executives did not embrace the services and values for which we stood. Rather they were looking for a way to find their next executive job and hoped by working for us a client would hire them. The point: it's difficult to sustain long term success if you're providing a service or product you truly don't intellectually and emotionally believe in. It's like trying to sell Fords while you show up for work every day driving a Toyota.

As a point of contrast, in my role as a rainmaker for The Hunter Group, I was not a professionally trained salesperson but ended up in this role because I believed wholeheartedly in the consulting and interim management services we provided and the results that could be achieved. I was thankful for the skills and talents our incredible team brought to our clients and prospective clients. I enthusiastically embraced what we did, I burned with passion, or a "fire in the belly" if you will. This opened doors for our company, and we won our share of projects. Once we did, we made sure serving our clients' needs was our number one focus and responsibility. Everything else naturally flowed from this and was successful as a result.

We later sold our company and we became part of the large consulting firm, Navigant Consulting. Here's one humorous story worth telling from my wonderful four years at Navigant. Our management team was presenting to a group of Wall Street investors. When it was my turn to speak I noticed the presenter before me went down the wrong aisle to get to her seat, so she had to backtrack. Well for some reason it triggered a thought, so I began my talk spontaneously off script.

I relayed a story of being at a client's office checking on the progress of our work when I got a call about a hospital in need of a turnaround. I was familiar with that hospital and its market and I absolutely knew we were the right firm for the job. I just needed to get there first and get in front of the CEO. So I excused myself from my client with their blessing and that of my team, and took off for the airport. I ran through the airport corridors dripping in sweat on a very hot summer day and finally got to the ticket counter, about out of breath. Once called to the counter by the agent he asked how he could help me. I said "I need to be on the very next flight you have to Los Angeles!" The man looked at me for a few seconds over the rim of his eye glasses and said "sir, you are in Los Angeles."

Hearing my story, the participants in this investor conference broke out in loud laughter! My boss, Bill Goodyear, the Chairman and CEO, was seated at a table to my far left facing the audience. He looked over at me standing at the lectern and asked if that was a true story. I said unfortunately it was!

I learned many months later from our then-chief operating officer that Mr. Goodyear loved telling that story as he traveled to our offices and markets across three continents because it demonstrated the passion (fire in the belly) of being alert to new opportunities while focusing on serving current clients.

Passion and perseverance in being able to carry out your business plan is something the Lord commands us to bring to our work, it is that important. Ponder these key work attributes from the Bible: desire, eagerness, willingness, giving and finishing. (2 Corinthians 8:10-12) And the capstone on the test of having "fire in the belly" is perhaps found in this verse: "excel in everything—in faith, in speech, in knowledge, in complete earnestness" in love for those you serve." (2 Corinthians 8:7)

Do we care this much about our customers and clients? Or is it mostly about the paycheck, bonuses, and meeting the company's numbers, no matter how they are achieved? Remember the proverb "the plans of the diligent lead to profit as surely as haste leads to poverty." (Proverbs 21:5) Do we go to work every day truly believing in our business and its products or services? Do we believe it enough to excel at what we do?

Adjust or abandon?

It has been attributed to former professional boxing champion, Mike Tyson, that "everyone has a plan 'til they get punched in the mouth," then out goes the plan![2]

Part of what goes into making a plan realistic is understanding everything is not going to go as desired. Being able to adjust to changing circumstances will determine if your plan continues to be realistic; otherwise it risks becoming irrelevant or obsolete.

Higher education is one industry that is under pressure to change. The value of a traditional college education is in question given the debt taken on by students and the difficulty many face in finding appropriate jobs. In addition, with the increase in online courses and degree programs there are simply too many colleges and universities in an environment of declining enrollment. Many higher education facilities will need to merge to maintain their mission. Some have but others will wait too long and likely face closure. For this industry "adjust or abandon" is front and center in their strategic planning.

One of the reasons I enjoy being a sports fan is the strategy part of sports. My son once treated me to a Philadelphia Eagles fan fest day in which half our time was spent on the practice field doing physical activities, such as passing, receiving or kicking the football. The remainder of our time was in the classroom critiquing strategy and tactics. I remember one class in particular where a former player was illustrating a replay of a key part of a game in which the Eagles faced their most detested rival, the Dallas Cowboys. Displayed on the screen was a specific defense the Eagles set up late in the game. However, the cornerback for the Eagles was not aware of the specific situation, failing to realize it was third down and long (about 20 yards). Stopping the Cowboys at this point would probably put the Eagles in position to win the game; however, the one player, not comprehending and adjusting to the situation, got beat on the play and the Cowboys went on to win the game.

Every leader can tell stories of things that did not go as planned, but the question is, what do we do at that point to stay true to our mission and plan? In the previous chapter we mentioned the Old Testament character Nehemiah, considered by some to be The Master of Business Administration (MBA). He prayed about his vision to rebuild the city walls of Jerusalem, and carried it further by defining the mission supported by a detailed strategic plan. Frankly, few outsiders thought this mission could be completed.

While carrying out the plan, things started to go wrong and external opposition arose from "competitors" or people who did not want to see his business plan succeed. Their antagonism started out as verbal gossip but then turned into real physical threats.

Nehemiah developed innovative ways to keep the plan on track while taking care of his people's needs. (Chapters 4 and 6) He reallocated resources (people) at vulnerable spots, formed teams, and provided equipment to protect what had been accomplished to date. In other words, he repositioned resources for the purpose of completing the work; he did not abandon the plan. His confidence was further strengthened because his people indeed had "fire in their belly;" they truly believed in the work they were doing as expressed with these words: "for the people worked with all their heart." (Nehemiah 4:6)

Those words are an amazing testimony, and all of us should ask ourselves if these same words can describe our own work ethic. Steady plodding and diligence bring about success. (Proverbs 10:4) Despite circumstances that were unexpected and certainly unwanted, Nehemiah's adjustments and the people's heart-felt belief in the mission and plan allowed the rebuilding project to be completed in the incredibly short time of fifty-two days. (Nehemiah 6:15) Nehemiah is a person every leader should take time to study.

Adjusting our plans challenges us to anticipate the future and discern if the so-called inevitable trends are indeed factual or merely business buzz filling the current news cycle. The leader's challenge is to stay ahead of the curve, making adjustments now to avoid more stressful or panic-like moves later.

Another Biblical mentor for us to consider in developing and adjusting plans is the Old Testament character Joseph, the youngest son of Jacob. He had a specific plan to weather an upcoming economic storm, in this case a famine, which was not even on anyone's radar, given the favorable economy. Joseph's plan of storing food supplies for future use was developed during good times. I'm sure many people thought he was probably a fatalist of sorts, but the king was so impressed by his plan he put him in charge of the country; in essence he became the chief operating officer. Joseph's plan saved the country when it was hit by extremely hard times. (Genesis 41) Joseph made adjustments in the good times in order for his country to remain viable during what amounted to an economic depression.

Thinking of alternative actions and exit strategies while things are seemingly going well is the mark of an excellent leader. Complacency, on the other hand, is a career killer.

Leaders like Nehemiah and Joseph remind me of the proverb that by wisdom a business is built, and through understanding it is sustained; a wise man has great power, and increases in strength. (Proverbs 24: 3,5) "In their hearts humans plan their course, but the Lord establishes their steps." (Proverbs 16:9) Plan wisely, adjust with foresight, and see what outcomes the Lord brings!

Chapter 6 Self-Assessment:
Planning: *How* Will We Accomplish Our Vision?

Reflections:

1. Do you have a good sense of the history of your company?
2. Is the history of your company part of the strategic dialogue?
3. Do you believe your company's plan is realistic given the competitive market?
4. Do you believe people see you as passionate about what your company does?
5. Are you confident in your own career direction?

Action Steps:

1. Critique how your segment of the business is doing:
    a. List two things going really well and answer, why are they going well?
    b. Are there assumptions about your business not steeped in reality? Work to correct them.
    c. List two things really worrying you. What can you do to adjust? Abandon?
2. Do you really believe in what your company does? Answer the following:

a. Would you or do you buy or use its product or services?

   b. Do you speak well of the company internally and externally?

   c. Do your company's values mirror your values?

3. In the opening paragraph of this chapter we used the story from Luke 14 where Jesus counseled that planning must account for the total cost (e.g. people, facilities, technology, supplies, time, etc.). As you plan the segment of the business (or your own household) for which you are responsible, have total costs been sufficiently accounted for? Decide what you would adjust and determine what might be missing in order for your business or household to remain viable.

Key Bible Verses: Read and contemplate 2 Corinthians 8: 7-12; Proverbs 16: 1-9; Proverbs 10:4; 19:21; 20: 18, 24; 21:5; finally read Psalm 37: 23-24.

Chapter 6: Footnotes

1. Joseph Lieberman, "A Divine Lesson in Governing," *The Wall Street Journal* (May 16, 2014).

2. Goodreads quotes, Mike Tyson, (https://www.goodreads.com/quotes/search?utf8=%9C%93&q=Mike+Tyson&committ+Search), accessed May 17, 2016.

Chapter 7
Priorities: Are We *Doing* What We Planned?

One thing I often do as a consultant is review an organization's strategic plan. Then as I meet people and observe the company in action it becomes clear where time and energy is spent. I ask myself, are the priorities as articulated in the company's plan actually carried out in a consistent matter? Too many times the stated priorities aren't where the majority of time and effort are being spent. Other priorities slip in and take over, or the seemingly recurring crisis of the day becomes consuming at the expense of strategic priorities.

A nurse from a neighboring state mailed me a memo sent to each employee in her organization. The hospital, though profitable, needed to make more money according to the CEO. Having a financial background, I understand a sufficient bottom line is required to keep any business going, be it tax-exempt or a taxable organization. But this memo was all about the numbers, a very long dissertation about bond ratings, margins, organizational alliances, etc., with the word "patient" being mentioned only once, and that was in context of a metric.

Such a memo, though well intended, likely did not win over the hearts and minds of nurses, doctors, housekeepers, cooks, etc. The impression the CEO communicated was that "numbers" are the most important thing. The central core of the hospital's purpose, taking care of patients, was never mentioned. Achieving the numbers seemed to be *the* overarching priority communicated to the employees. Remember, people judge us by our actions, not our intentions.

A case in point of numbers actually being a priority with actions matching plan is associated with the founder of Ikea, the furniture retailer. "The company doesn't place as its first priority that the products shall look nice; low prices take priority over everything else." To set the example, Ingvar Kamprad, the founder of IKEA, would reuse tea bags, fly economy class, and use public transportation.[1] Having the lowest prices was his company's most important priority and he lived that out through his daily actions.

Updating priorities

If people are not updated on the current priorities of an organization, their own "to-do" lists become a blur as new challenges are added while nothing is taken away or at least re-prioritized. An unending list of priorities becomes not only daunting, but impractical to effectively manage.

In one consulting experience I observed a financially challenged health care system with about twenty-five priorities. When a company has that many priorities it usually means little, if anything, of substance is getting done, so it was no wonder they were in trouble. As they reorganized to get control, more and more decisions were made by a growing and bloated corporate headquarters, thus slowing down processes at the local entities.

One of my business partners gave me this quote about ten years ago: "We trained hard, but it seemed that every time we were beginning to form up into teams we would be reorganized. I was to learn later in life that we tend to meet any new situation by reorganizing; and a wonderful method it can be for creating the illusion of progress while producing confusion, inefficiency and demoralization." That quote is attributed to Petronius Arbiter who lived in the first century AD.[2] Some things haven't changed much in corporate life.

When I coach executives, I like to ask them to list their top priorities, what they believe they are being held responsible for accomplishing. Then I ask them to list their organization's priorities. Finally, I ask them to study their own priorities against the organization's priorities. If they don't see a correlation between their efforts and the goals of the organization there is a disconnect; their priorities need to be clarified and adjusted.

The CEO of Ryder Systems (you are likely familiar with Ryder rental trucks) tried to communicate five strategic priorities to his employees; however, he used so much complex "financial speak" during his one-hour staff presentation he eventually noticed the blank stares when he asked the group if they understood. He had lost them. He later adjusted and reduced a one-hundred-page slide show down to two-pages which drove home to his staff where Ryder stood and what it needed to do in the industry to succeed.[3]

Here's the bottom line: don't assume people know what's in your head. Communicate *frequently* the most important priorities in a matter people will *clearly* understand. Communicate what needs to be done, what resources are being deployed to do it, and the timelines or milestones for completion. Your team members will appreciate that kind of decisiveness and directness.

Competing priorities

There is a great story in the Old Testament book of Haggai about competing priorities. God's priority was for his people to rebuild the temple. But the people consumed their time with their houses, gardens and taking care of satisfying themselves, as described this way: "you have planted much, but have harvested little. You eat, but never have enough. You drink, but never have your fill. You put on clothes, but are not warm. You earn wages, only to put them in a purse with holes in it." (Haggai 1:6) Wow, some people think the Bible is out of date. We should all meditate on this verse. God's admonition on priorities, expressed twice in this chapter, was to "give careful thoughts to your ways," (Haggai 1:5, 7) because competing priorities often become confused priorities, with little to show in terms of substantive results.

As another example, I think competing priorities were a significant factor in compromising the performance and public acceptance of much of the Obama administration's two terms. Coming into office and faced with serious economic challenges and terrorist threats, "the President's focus on health care allowed the public to infer that his mind was not focused on our security. He frittered his attention on issues that were secondary and tertiary—climate change, health care—while al Qaeda moved and the country's economic system stuttered. A lack of focus breeds bureaucratic complacency, complacency gives rise to slovenliness, slovenliness results in serious trouble if not outright danger."[4]

He is certainly not the only President of either party whose effectiveness was detoured by competing priorities. The current President, Donald Trump, is certainly struggling to get definition and acceptance of his administration's priorities in such areas as health care (trying to bend the cost curve while increasing options for coverage) and border security (providing more security between Mexico and the USA amidst the conflicts of the political and financial risks of doing so). If this can happen to Presidents, then it certainly behooves all leaders to be acutely conscious of the confusion brought on by competing priorities.

When I was a managing director for a division of a public company, Navigant Consulting, our priority was to win consulting engagements with hospitals. Another group within our company worked to win jobs with insurance companies. This would cause consternation because often hospitals and insurance companies are at odds with each other. This frequently caused our company a conflict as to whom to serve. At times we would have to walk away from potential work because we were conflicted due to competing priorities, which sometimes resulted in a terrible waste of our people's time, talent and energy. It was demoralizing to win work only to turn it down.

Priorities that really move an organization can be few but need to be crystal clear, highly focused, practical and embraced by those assigned to carry them out (with a "fire in the belly"). In my consulting business we focused on winning jobs at health systems or large hospitals to provide performance improvement services and/or interim management. These priorities correlated with our vision, mission and the strategic plan. There are plenty of goals most organizations would like to achieve, but one imperative of a strategic plan is to identify and assign resources to carry out what is deemed most important to the mission. What actions substantially move the needle towards accomplishing your mission? Competing priorities can easily creep in. It takes relentless fortitude for leaders to keep the focus on what is truly of utmost importance.

Substituting priorities

As mentioned in the previous chapter, one reason I think strategic plans get tossed to the side is because implementing those plans often requires some very difficult actions. Things might look good on paper, but putting plans into action guarantees at one time or another certain stakeholder groups will be adversely affected.

For instance, I have worked with clients in the healthcare and educational sectors that long ago should have merged or even closed, but local politicians viewed the affected employees as votes and fought vigorously against merging or closing. Almost always the protraction of an obvious direction or solution only makes the later required action more painful to execute. We delay or postpone the more appropriate intervention, relegating it to the future by substituting another priority which is less difficult or controversial at the moment.

Here is a Biblical story that perhaps accents the pitfalls in substituting priorities. Just about everyone knows the story of Jonah being swallowed by a big fish and living in it for three days before being coughed up on shore. However, what perhaps a number of people miss is the reason for this episode. Jonah had been given a charge to work in a certain city, Nineveh. (Today this city is known as Mosul, the second largest city in Iraq; the tomb of Jonah was destroyed just a few years ago by ISIS).[5] However, he did not like the assignment because he frankly did not like the city. To put it bluntly, Jonah simply did not like the people of Nineveh. (Jonah 4:1,2) He really did not want to see them succeed.

I think many of us have had Jonah moments—we don't like a competitor, or worse, we don't like someone within our own team or company. Frankly, rather than help them we wouldn't mind seeing them fail. This was Jonah's position. So, he substituted another city,

Tarshish figuring he was still doing God's work; he just picked another venue. Upon heading for his self-appointed replacement assignment, Jonah was intercepted by God who intervened with a teachable moment, aka the fish story, redirecting the prophet's focus so he would stick with the "Plan." God's priority was Nineveh and in the end, of course, it prevailed. (Jonah 1:17) If we substitute or replace priorities from our original plan from a basis of fear, resentment, dislike, or anger, the critical take-away to contemplate is that *substituting activity does not equal purposeful accomplishment.*

Here is a business story to further forewarn you about the pitfalls of substituting priorities. Our organization once gained a job because another consulting firm was substituting activity in place of purposeful and timely accomplishment. The hospital needed to cut costs; however, its consulting firm at that time instructed management to lay off only a handful of people each payroll period. Perhaps the consultants feared the adverse publicity the hospital would suffer by announcing a large number of layoffs.

One day a partner of mine and I were asked to meet with the corporate Chief Financial Officer of the system which owned this hospital. He explained the layoff process taking place at this particular division and described it as being like "water torture." The anxiety caused by this protracted process was like taking off a band-aid by the millimeter instead of just making one swipe and getting it over with. The employees knew what was happening so the lengthy process was demoralizing.

Business Practices, Biblical Promises

The CFO wanted to know how we would handle this labor cost problem. We laid out our preferred approach, which was to identify the required workforce reduction to bring about financial stability and implement the plan in one move. He asked us to meet him at 9:00 a.m. at the hospital, whereupon he fired the other firm and introduced us as the new team who would assist management with the turnaround. The actions required were quite obvious; however, the previous consulting firm substituted a protracted time frame in place of immediate remedial action hoping the magnitude of the cost cutting might not be so visible.

Priorities become personal: faith, family and work

A company's priorities and our business priorities become personal because they cause us to make choices. Can we faithfully embrace our company's work and priorities? I once worked for a company whose priorities and methods of achieving those objectives were ones I could not enthusiastically embrace, so I left. The pressure to reclassify expenses to meet budget targets was just one such example. Meeting company financial targets can cause people to make decisions that ultimately they will come to regret. Can you embrace what your company stands for and how it goes about accomplishing its work?

We honor God in our work by carrying out our responsibilities faithfully for our employer, as long as that work is not contrary to the teachings of the scriptures. We are to be mindful of the bigger picture, eternity, not fixating on things here on earth that one day will mean nothing. (Colossians 3: 1-4) God is forever, everything on earth is not.

Business priorities become personal because our work life can consume us, as it does so many people in the United States and other countries of the world. But work does not encompass all of life, nor should it. Work is important, yes, as it's an opportunity to live out God's desired purpose for us, but it should not consume our entire beings.

God asked each of us to serve Him first, to do His will. (Matthew 22: 37-39) In fact, the apostle Paul puts the question squarely to us: "Am I now trying to win the approval of human beings, or of God? Or am I trying to please people?" (Galatians 1:10) Life is short, so this same apostle counsels us to "live a life worthy of the calling you have received." (Ephesians 4: 1) Seek God's direction on where He can best use your gifts and talents.

Yet our business priorities are not supposed to take away from our family priorities. That is a lot easier said than done in our culture. I for one do not write about this from a position of strength, but rather one of weakness, having failed often in appropriately prioritizing family over work. There are many days of my own life when I prioritized work over family that I regret and will not get back, and I suspect that I am not alone. Chances are you have been or might be in this struggle right now. As one author, Peggy Noonan, so ably puts it in her book, *The Time of Our Lives*, "does family life spill over into work life? No. Work life spills over into family life."[6]

Business Practices, Biblical Promises

We don't take our daughters or sons for walks at work, but we have no problem being interrupted at our child's sporting event to take a business call. I did that so often it made me sick then and makes me nearly ill now when I think about it, a poor choice of my own priorities. I still remember one day when I was to be at an ice skating recital for my two kids, Pam and Kevin. I ended up missing it because of a "crisis" involving doctors arguing over money and medical equipment. To this day, I regret forfeiting a family priority while mediating a selfish business agenda. I can't tell you how many of my son's basketball games I missed. This kind of misplacement of a family priority is not a feather in my resume or on my LinkedIn profile.

In fact, as I worked toward wrapping up this book I've wrestled with a decision involving priority of business versus family. If that were not enough, I'm talking about a "volunteer" position in the business world; it's not even a paid job.

For the last six months of 2018 I had been serving as the Chair of the Board of Directors for a health system in Maryland affiliated with the University of Maryland, the Upper Chesapeake Health System. The two-hospital system serves a county that sits at the top of the Chesapeake Bay, Harford County, with a population of about two- hundred and fifty thousand. I've been filling the unexpired term of the previous board chair who had served in that role for over twenty years. Even though my wife has some chronic health challenges and needs my assistance in carrying out some of life's duties she was supportive of my taking on this role. Having worked with executives and boards in various industries, including healthcare, she was familiar with the demands of the role and knew it had important purpose but with a limited time frame.

Here is the dilemma that unfolded as I was heading toward completing my term. I had been asked by several key board members if I would accept a full term as chair of the board, which would mean two more years; furthermore, given the by-laws at that time did not address term limits, there was the chance this could turn out to be an even longer commitment.

The allure of business can be so strong (even in volunteer work) it draws you into thinking you are serving a greater good by making it *the* priority. I'm embarrassed to say, but must honestly disclose, I wrestled with this decision, despite my wife's need and desire I spend more time at home. Many will understand the adrenalin lift that comes from working in a field you love, in my case, the healthcare industry. The *intellectual stimulation* of working with people who are also passionate about service—doctors, nurses, technicians, housekeepers, cooks, security personal, fellow board members—all wanting to make a difference. is fulfilling. That sense of collaboration and teamwork in an industry where teamwork is critical to the success of caring for patients provides an internal heartfelt lift when performed well.

There is also the drive a *challenge* presents, not only to make a difference in areas you think you are comfortable tackling, but in those where unknown crises are bound to occur, to see if you'll succeed —there is a certain curiosity and thrill about being stretched beyond your comfort zone.

There are the internal juices provided by *competition*, to see if you can beat the best, become the best, or stay at the top. In fact, when I ran several consulting firms and served in the role as "rainmaker" (the guy who had to bring the work in the company door) that feeling of winning an engagement was so high it was the equivalent of hitting a home run or scoring a touchdown---and most times we were beating out firms much larger than ours. You can get a little heady if you're not careful.

And there is that sense of *accomplishment* you get in business, when you succeed at a really difficult challenge, perhaps save a client from failure, or propel them to significantly higher achievement. It is the unique feeling of having made a contribution that made a significant difference in the life of people and an organization. One of those times for me was saving jobs. Numerous times I would go to the CEO of a large system and let them know it would be a mistake to fire the executive(s) at a certain hospital, as they were about to pull the trigger. Most times these vulnerable executives didn't even know I saved their jobs—but I knew, and God knew, so I got great satisfaction out of that accomplishment.

You get the sense of the draw of work, be it traditional business, ministry, sports, military…it applies even to volunteer work. If you're asked to serve as a board chair of anything, it feels like a pretty big deal in its own right. So here I am with my wife's health challenges still contemplating if I should agree to be willing to serve a full term as Board Chair. Six months was one thing, but the idea of at least two years or more at our age did not sit well with my wife Connie in terms of which priority to choose.

When Connie and I discussed this issue a few times she was honest and blunt enough to say she was praying I would not take this role, while I was praying for God's will—or at least I thought I was. Her prayer may seem pretty selfish, but it really wasn't. Looking back, I see my wife was trying to save me from myself. What does that mean? My wife more than anyone else on earth knows my heartfelt regrets from several decades of extensive business travel and work hours that took me away from my family. She also knows how serious I take a leadership role and what I put into it. If, for example, a board chair should spend an average of twenty hours a month in his role, well, I would invest forty. She knows I believe the job must be done right and it must be done well; she knows my M.O.

As I prayed about this decision and asked God for wisdom it dawned on me why my wife prayed the way she did. God brought back to my mind that I made a promise to Him and to myself that I would do better at controlling my calendar so as to provide more availability to be with my wife, kids and grandkids in our blended family.

If you're a grandparent you already know that a special relationship exists with your grandchild. As a board member from a college once said to me, "Larry do you know why grandparents and grandkids have such a special bond?" I said, "no Fred, tell me why."

Business Practices, Biblical Promises

He responded, "Grandparents and grandkids have a special relationship because they share a common enemy." You laugh because you got that and you know there is a kernel of truth to that observation!

So you can probably understand my wife's reaction was not only for her own physical and emotional needs. It was equally, and probably more so, to save me from taking on something that would only lead to deeper regrets than I already accumulated over the length of a long career—one that most people would deem "successful" but cost me heavily because I placed business over family. Those regrets are mirrored back to me often as I watch the incredible work ethic of our kids and grandkids, and the struggles they now have prioritizing family and work. Remember, your kids are far more likely to mirror your behavior than they are your good intentions.

As I wrestled with this it became clear that my wife and I are entering a season of life where age and health require sufficient availability to be able to help each other, plus enjoy family gatherings, recitals, graduations, sporting events, family vacations, etc., while health and time still permit them.

Ultimately, I declined the opportunity to be considered for a full term as board chair with peace about the decision. That peace was further strengthened when I recommended to our nominating committee the name of a man I was confident would do an excellent job, and do it better than me, which would benefit our organization and our community.

Yes, the allure of business success is so strong that I went through this kind of spiritual mud wrestling before finally prioritizing family, especially my wife, over work—and volunteer work at that!

Many women and men are conflicted about family and work priorities. The CEO of the large insurance and consulting company, Marsh & McLennan, was recently quoted saying, "Your kids are only young once, and you can't get that back. If I have any regrets, it's that one." [7] Many of us know the pain of this regret.

The CEO of Choice Hotels learned the hard way about this issue when his marriage ended in divorce. He offers this wise advice for all decision makers, especially leaders: "It's critical for the CEO to set the tone. If he doesn't, there's a secret kind of code, 'if you take vacation, you're not as serious an executive'."[8]

I departed one of my CEO roles with twelve unused weeks of vacation. That was not only bad for my family, it set a poor example for other leaders in our organization.

Brenda Barnes was a high-ranking executive of Pepsi Company, heading up their North American beverage division. She was in line to become CEO. In 1997 she resigned because she wanted more engaged time with her three children who ranged in ages from seven to ten-years-old. Her resignation caused quite a buzz as reporters and television personalities requested interviews with her as to why she would make such a radical decision to change her priorities.

Later, when asked if women could have it all she said "no," women had to make a choice. When her children were older she accepted the opportunity in 2004 to become President of Sara Lee Corp., and was promoted to CEO a year later. When asked if she regretted the six and one-half year gap in her resume she responded, "I would do it a million times over."[9] Her priorities changed with seasons of life; she was clearly a woman of substantive wisdom. Ms. Barnes passed away in 2017 at the age of sixty-three. Life is short, our priorities matter. Priorities are choices.

The family unit in our country is broken, experiencing high levels of social chaos and dysfunction, giving rise to our individual and collective needs to come to grips with personal and work priorities.

The two-parent family is shrinking to the point where one in four American children live in one-parent families, twice the rate of those in Europe. More than twenty percent of these kids will live in long-term poverty compared to two percent in two-parent families. In America, about forty percent of our kids are growing up without a father actively involved in their lives, and that rate is an alarming seventy-two percent for African-American children.[10] The effect of the change of our family dynamics is underreported while alternatives seemingly centered on political ideology are presented as solutions to our growing family woes. Our minority communities have been impacted the hardest.[11]

One of the reasons I so respect the former football coach Tony Dungy is that he did not pull the usual coach thing of living in the office at the stadium and sleeping on the couch. He made it a goal to be with his family each evening and gave each of his coaches and players the same opportunity to make family a priority without compromising key business priorities. He allowed the players' children to be around the practice facilities on Saturdays. He also expected his players to be involved with the community. He understands strong families make us better people in all roles of our lives. I was a late learner to this, but I pray you will not be!

A professional baseball player, Adam LaRoche, thought he had an understanding with the Chicago White Sox that his fourteen-year-old son could be with him every day in the clubhouse; however, during spring training in 2016 the club ordered him to significantly reduce the amount of time his son was with the team. LaRoche immediately retired rather than be separated from his son, walking away from a thirteen-million-dollar contract. Time with his son at a critical point of his teenage life was more important than pocketing millions of dollars.[12]

Here is a biblical story to put a capstone on this point. Solomon, considered a wise and great king, conscripted people in Israel to help build the temple. He drafted enough people so that when they went out of town to work they did so for one month, but then came back and spent two months working in their home area so they could have sufficient time with their families. (I Kings 5: 13,14) He understood the strength of his nation, like all nations, was in correlation to the strength of its families.

I can relate to this story because in my own career, traveling five days a week for over two decades cost my family and me precious time and memories. That intense travel schedule, which translated into significant family separation, was *the* major factor in my retiring from corporate life and going into my own consulting and executive coaching business. My priorities as a husband, father, grandfather, and business executive were better fulfilled by a position in which I could control the number of clients I accepted along with its correlating travel schedule.

In summary, business and career priorities become very personal because they impact all aspects of our lives. Absent a laser-like focus on our priorities each day, we end up with conflict and tension. Perhaps this is one reason Jesus said we must take up His cross *daily*. (Luke 9:23) Our daily activities are indicative of whom or what is truly first in our hearts and minds.

Chapter 7 Self-Assessment:
Priorities: Are We *Doing* What We Planned?

Reflections:

1. Does your boss communicate frequently your organization's priorities?
2. Do you communicate your unit's priorities often to your people?
3. Have you ever experienced competing priorities in your work?
4. Do you feel work life encroaches on family life?

Action Steps:

1. List the top three work priorities *you* have at this time. List the top three priorities of your *company*. Do you see a strong correlation between the two lists? If not, immediately clarify what you are doing and any conflicts, along with confirming your organization's top priorities, then re-prioritize your own.
2. Priorities don't remain stagnant. When is the last time your boss verbalized the company's priorities? Write down what they were.
3. What is the last thing you missed with your kids because of a work or related social events? Write about the experience.

Business Practices, Biblical Promises

   a. Answer the question, what will you do to change this next time?

   b. Contemplate the risk of not making changes, as those translate later into regrets.

Key Bible Verses: Read and contemplate Psalm 90:12; Matthew 22:37-40; Ephesians 4:1; 5:15-17; 6:5-9; and Colossians 3:1-4.

Chapter 7 Footnotes

1. James R. Hagerty, "Ikea Founder Built Retailer By Keeping It Simple," *The Wall Street Journal,* (February 3-4, 2018), p. A9.
2. Goodreads.com, Petronius Arbiter Quotes. (http://www.goodreads.com/author/quotes/92278), accessed January 27, 2016.
3. Joann S. Lublin, "Rookie CEO's Face a Steep Learning Curve," *The Wall Street Journal,* (July 25, 2014), p. B7.
4. Peggy Noonan, "The Risk of Catastrophic Victory," *The Wall Street Journal,* (January 9-10, 2010), p. A13.
5. Benjamin Blech, "An Ancient Tomb Meets a Modern Horror." *The Wall Street Journal* (August 1, 2014).
6. Peggy Noonan, *The Time of Our Lives,* (New York: Twelve, Hachette Book Group, 2015), p. 197.
7. Rachel Feintzeig, "Male CEOs Detail Their Work-Life Rules." *The Wall Street Journal* (June 15, 2016), p. B1
8. Ibid, p.B5.

9. James R. Hagerty, "Obituaries, Brenda Barnes," *The Wall Street Journal*, (January 21-22, 2017), p. A13.
10. Focus on the Family Radio Program, Weekend Edition, WDAC Radio, Lancaster, Pa, June 18, 2016.
11. Robert Maranto and Michael Crouch, "Ignoring an Inequality Culprit: Single-Parent Families," *The Wall Street Journal*, (April 21, 2014).
12. New York Post, "MLB player retires because team says he can't bring son to clubhouse" (http://www.foxnews.com/sports/2016/03/17/mlb-player-retires-because-team-says-cant-bring-son-to-clubhouse.print.html) accessed May 1, 2016.

Chapter 8

Metrics and Milestones: *Measuring Our Progress*

In writing about the former and great New York Yankee baseball pitcher Mariano Rivera following his retirement in 2013, writer Jason Gay of the *Wall Street Journal* opined that Rivera's most remarkable accomplishment of his career was his *dignity*. "Dignity is an unusual evasive value in modern sports. There is no metric for it, no statistical standard." This comment is seemingly contrary to the culture of baseball given its obsession with scorecards, metrics and statistics. The author goes on to say that "dignity won't assure you success the way the world defines it, because those who aspire to work in such fashion will have their performance, commitment and character scrutinized and questioned—it's really hard work."[1]

Most organizations go to great lengths to statistically measure how they are doing. Data has never been so readily available or so central to our business culture. Data mining and business intelligence are so important they constitute their own industry. We want to know not only how we measure against our plan, but how we stand versus our competitors. Everyone wants information because we want to get an edge. You name an industry and those companies are measuring their performance; it's as if scorecards have become a compulsion.

Wall Street looks forward to quarterly earnings calls of publicly traded companies so they can find out if a company has met the performance standards of industry analysts; the outcomes of these financial updates affect the price of the stock before the earnings call is even finished. The use of data by baseball teams to track performance and measure the value of individual players was so prevalent it became the core theme of a hit book and movie, *Money Ball.* Mega churches are looking at numbers on how they can keep growing—some dropping programs deemed of lesser value so they can add yet another church campus in efforts to attract hundreds or thousands of additional congregants.

It's wonderful that so much data is available to measure progress against our plan and motivate us to improve performance. After all, doing something with this information is one way of judging our progress and perhaps distinguishing ourselves. Nearly every one of us has some role in the generation of information and data. This data gets rolled up into a series of agreed upon statistics and dollar values for which our business unit or our company is judged against the plan and budget. Let's be honest, anyone who has a role in generating numbers faces his or her own pressures. Meeting monthly, quarterly and annual targets causes considerable fretting for millions of leaders as well as those affected by the outcomes of these measures. Often, much is at stake; sometimes our paychecks, bonuses, or even whether or not we keep our job are on the line.

   Speaking of jobs, an agency in Tampa whose primary function is to help people find jobs suspended its CEO after it became known that it inflated the numbers of the people it supposedly helped to find employment.[2] The agency, CareerSource, listed people who apparently never used its services because higher numbers meant more government funding.

   I've had experiences with companies which, upon their initial internal review of monthly results, gather leaders together in person, or by phone or video conference and then go through a "dialing for dollars" exercise attempting to determine if something was missed or if some "adjustment" can reasonably be made to improve company numbers before results are officially released. Pressures for favorable numbers has the Security and Exchange Commission keeping a close eye on the latest trend of businesses to report metrics that do not comply with generally accepted accounting practices, but which tend to serve the purpose of making a company's performance look better.[3]

   So, given today's culture, could the Bible possibly have anything to say about data, information, metrics, measures and scorecards? You bet it does, to use a financial pun!

Liberal accounting policies...everyone does it, right?

In 1984 Aaron Beam and Richard Scrushy, founded a company called HealthSouth Corp. Mr. Beam was a CPA who would become the chief financial officer (CFO) while his partner became the high-profile CEO. Within ten years they built a billion-dollar company that provided rehabilitation services in all fifty states. The pressure to meet plans and expectations seeded the acts of fraud that commenced in 1996. Mr. Beam retired as CFO in 1997, but the web of deception had taken root and spread like cancer. The fraud continued through several successor CFOs and didn't surface until 2003. The fraudulent act was technically quite simple, as "adjustments" were made to accounting debits and credits. But as the months and years rolled on, the company required 120,000 fraudulent journal entries *per quarter* "to make the numbers work."[4]

Prison time was meted out to a number of those involved, including Mr. Beam. After losing all of his possessions he decided one way to rebuild his life was to share his story with others hoping to prevent them from repeating a scheme he never thought he would be part of himself. In Aaron's words, "when you work for a company that stresses profits at all costs, it is a potentially destructive situation. You must seriously consider the company's values when taking a job. Above all else, be prepared to walk away from an otherwise good job if you are asked to commit or be a party to fraud."[5]

If you think your company will take care of you for doing something "minor" or making modest adjustments to be later reconciled or reversed, let me assure you that will not happen no matter what your boss or any other leader might tell you.

Once I worked with a company where one job site had some statistical reporting errors—not fraud, but mistakes on the classification of labor hours of work performed on site. A local newspaper reporter, who was often looking for something sensational with this particular firm, attempted to blow-up this misclassification issue into something much bigger than the facts warranted. The company commenced its own investigation of the incident and informed the leaders on the project to get their own attorneys. For those professionals informed of their need to hire their own legal help, it was a wakeup call on the limits of "company loyalty". Not long after the dust settled each of those leaders left. Even in the absence of purposeful wrong doing, the stark reality of legal exposure and the appearance of dishonesty can be very costly to one's professional reputation, let alone possible financial consequences.

If you don't think you could face such pressure "to make the numbers work" supporting your company's strategic plan and budget, consider this case reported in *The Wall Street Journal*:

> "Three consecutive Toshiba Corp. chief executives fueled more than one billion dollars in accounting irregularities by setting unrealistic profit targets and demanding that subordinates meet them" according to an independent panel hired by the company. Managers were pressured to

achieve high sales targets, such pressure often coming before the end of the quarter or the fiscal year. The corporate culture was described as one in "which it was impossible to go against the intentions of superiors".[6]

Another instructive case involves, of all companies, a law firm. A number of employees comprised of operations, accounting and back-office staff from the now collapsed law firm of Dewey & LeBoeuf, LLP allegedly did the bidding of some corporate officers to "hide the firm's true financial condition from creditors, investors, auditors and even partners of the firm." This manipulation was carried out over a period of years and involved such wrongdoing as fabricating invoices. The star witness at the first trial was the firm's former finance director who admitted the fraud was cooked up over a steak dinner in Midtown Manhattan in December, 2008. In March of 2014 the district attorney handed down a 106-count indictment. Most charges were dismissed due to the complexity of the case and the inability to prove the charges. Nevertheless, seven employees pleaded guilty to participating in the fraud.[7]

The pressure to keep our own jobs in part by keeping the boss, outside bankers, analysts, or politicians happy is something we must guard against.

I will always remember a person I had to confront in a fraud case we uncovered on behalf of a client. She told me how very nervous she was the first time she committed such an act, but that thereafter each malfeasance got easier. The fraud went undetected for eight years. The word "sin" is not a politically correct word in our culture, but the New Testament book of James tells it straight: "every man is tempted when he is drawn away of his own lust, and enticed; then when lust has conceived, it brings forth sin; and sin, when it is finished, brings forth death." (James 1:14,15)[8] In this case, death is that sick, empty feeling of comprehending that one's inappropriate, unethical or illegal actions were not worth the outcome…or the end didn't justify the means. The realization of how far we have strayed from God's preferred way to live can indeed be humbling and often very costly.

Is it about process or results…or both?

The Old Testament book of Leviticus can be a laborious read, but it is basically a book instructing the people of Israel how to offer various types of sacrifices. It is detailed because God wanted the process done in a certain way for each type of sacrifice. It was more than just about the end result; the process of how one gets to the end was important enough that God put an emphasis on it. How and why we do something reveals our motives and what's in our hearts.

In one instructive moment, Aaron's two sons took a short cut in the process and performed an unauthorized procedure (violating the prescribed process for offering incense), which literally resulted in their deaths. (Leviticus 10:1,2) God wants us to understand He is holy, and doing things right is the best way to live, even if it is not expedient to our liking or our boss's desires. God's scorecard, metrics and standards were set way back thousands of years ago and apply to our day with words like, "do not use dishonest standards when measuring" and "use honest scales and honest weights." (Leviticus 19:35,36)

A few years ago (2014) on one given day, eighteen people were arrested who worked at the state owned Brazilian oil giant Petroleo Brasileiro SA. These people, along with others, were charged with a scam involving bribery and money-laundering that moved millions of dollars from the oil firm into the pockets of executives, employees, politicians and contractors. Part of how the fraud was perpetrated was through inflating the price of the work performed by the company.[9] (In late September of 2018 the oil company settled this investigation by agreeing to pay nearly a billion dollars to U.S. and Brazilian authorities. It is considered one of the largest scandals ever uncovered).[10]

The same day the news of the oil company scheme hit the papers and websites, Hertz, the rental car company, announced it would restate its financial results for the three previous years. They admitted "its accounting issues ran even deeper" than originally thought, since the firm had revealed the detection of accounting errors six months prior to this announcement.[11] Again, on this very same day an audit at the University of Maryland Eastern Shore could not account for a $25,000 grant, thus it was referred to the criminal division.[12] From this same newspaper that same day, a real estate businessman was reported to have defrauded seven million dollars from investors for his own personal use.[13] Four fraud stories emerged from a quick scan of one day's news in just a couple of newspapers!

But these "sins" aren't only regarding dollars and numbers; they can also be about scorecards. In 2018, six executives of the accounting firm KPMG were charged with fraud and conspiracy. The scheme involved executives acquiring advance information from a government regulatory body on which specific clients would be part of the regulators' audit or annual inspection. "That information would have enabled KPMG to better prepare for the inspections, resulting in an important report card of the firm's performance."[14]

In other words, by knowing which clients were going to be reviewed, KPMG compromised the objectivity of the inspections, as the advance information gave them an unauthorized inside edge on better preparing for the reviews.

The importance of *how* results are achieved can be illustrated by a true event that took place in the early days of the church not long after Christ's resurrection. The early Christians were living in such a unity of mission that they shared liberally among themselves, especially to those who had need.

One couple, Ananias and his wife, Sapphira, sold a piece of property so they could give *all* the proceeds to the church. However, the husband decided to keep some of the money for himself, and did so with his wife's full knowledge. They brought the remaining money to the church leaders as if it represented the entire proceeds of the transaction. In two startling moments that caused immense fear among the early Christians, the husband and wife, within a short time span of their dishonest actions, each collapsed to their immediate deaths. (Acts 5: 1-11) God wanted the early believers to learn a memorable lesson: again, *how* things are done is important to Him, because how we achieve results indeed reveals our motives.

Too Big to Fail?

General Electric (GE) is a household name around the world. One might think it too big to fail. But GE's financial performance is considered weak at this time and its reputation is that of "a serial tweaker of financial disclosures" as its accounting practices have come under review by the Securities and Exchange Commission.[15] With its performance continuing to be at variance with investor expectations and its stock price depressed, the company removed its CEO in October 2018 after only fourteen months on the job.

Think of big company names which trigger the thought "crime" or "fraud," e.g., Enron, Tyco, WorldCom, Global Crossing, Wells Fargo, Volkswagen, as well as others that likely come into your mind. As the Bible states, "Bad company corrupts good character....come back to your senses." (1 Corinthians 15: 33, 34)   Something is clearly wrong when companies that are pillars of the community, region, country or even the world are thought to be too important, and thus, too big to fail, only to be brought down by greed.

The late Michael Novak, author of *The Spirit of Democratic Capitalism*, was once asked why capitalism is good and he responded, "Of all the systems devised by man it is the one most likely to lift the poor out of poverty." But as he expounded on this thought, he stated capitalism "requires an underlying moral edifice. Without it nothing works; with it all is possible; it requires a knowledge that business can contribute to community and family; it requires 'a sense of sin,' a sense of right and wrong."[16]

Many people, especially young people, have lost trust in our most significant institutions—churches, business, banks, courts, housing, schools, media, healthcare, the list goes on. We fail to connect moral decline with the relentless campaign to remove God and His standards from the fabric of every aspect of our lives. We cannot correct spiritual or social ills by continuing to become even more godless, but this is where we as a society are apparently heading. We have lost that sense of right versus wrong. The breakdown of the family is one example. As courts, legislatures and society redefine family, one is hard pressed to see reference or reverence to the Bible or God in such debates. As we remove God from the fabric of our families, businesses and government, the devastating consequences have become more evident. The size of our various institutions doesn't cover up our moral decline, nor does size inoculate a business from failure.

The size of our company, our paycheck, or job title does not impress the Lord. He does not buy into the "too big to fail" mantra. God reminds us that our talents and our jobs are not of our own making nor do they provide our ultimate security. It is God that gives each of us the ability to work and produce a living. (Deuteronomy 8:17, 18) He puts us in a position to do good toward others. Are we doing good for others, or is our work mainly about serving ourselves?

We have the opportunity to hold our talents and our jobs up to Biblical standards which have meaning and value beyond the whim of current political, business or cultural expediency.

In fact, God tells us not to despise or look down on smaller sizes. In the book of Judges, God had Gideon pare down his army from 32,000 to 300. (Judges 7:1-8) God wanted Gideon and his team to have no doubt the military victory they achieved had nothing to do with outsizing the competition and everything to do with His mighty power. Size often produces a false sense of invincibility and arrogance.

The best company I ever worked for and eventually ran, The Hunter Group, was a small boutique consulting firm. On any given day we would win projects competing against nationally and internationally well-known large public and private enterprises. The Lord rejoices and blesses that which is done right and honorably, regardless of its size!

Debt

Debt is a relevant metric every company pays attention to, as should you and I regarding not only our business life, but our own personal finances.

Most businesses pay attention to the amount of their debt compared to their equity and cash positions. When a company takes on debt to finance its operations it signs onto a series of agreements, called covenants, in which the borrower agrees to run the business in a way that complies with these covenants. The reason for these agreements is that the lender wants to be sure the business remains profitable enough for their loan to be repaid within the agreed time frame.

For instance, when my partners and I bought our company, The Hunter Group, from its original founders, the agreement was to pay off our loan in six years. One of the covenants the bank required of us as new owners was to forego salary increases while the loan was outstanding. This was one of several reasons we all worked hard to successfully pay off the loan in half of the original time frame.

If a business fails to comply with one or more of these loan agreements the lender has the right to take action against it. Whether it's your company or your own personal financial situation, one key takeaway to ponder is what the Bible says regarding debt: "the borrower is a slave to the lender." (Proverbs 22:7) A business can lose flexibility when it takes on debt, especially if it struggles to meet the repayment terms or covenants.

Recently I met with the chairman of the board of a Christian school. The school had violated its loan covenants several times. Finally, after yet another violation, the bank called in the loan, meaning they wanted it paid off immediately. The headmaster was immediately relieved of his duties. Understanding and complying with loan covenants you or your company make with a lender is imperative to your financial health and well-being.

I once had a significant role with a client which in hindsight is a bit humorous, but the banks certainly did not see it that way at the time. This hospital had debt spread among three international banks with an Asian financial institution being the lead lender. Our company was hired because the organization was in "technical" default of its loan agreement, meaning it had enough cash to make principal and interest payments for the moment, but not enough cash and financial strength as required by the bank's covenants. Thus, the ability to continue to repay the debt was in question from the bank's point of view.

The organization had completed building a new tower to house patients, which the hospital assumed would produce additional revenues to meet its debt agreements; however, there was a problem. The day the lead bank's officials arrived to discuss the loan covenant violations, the new building was totally empty. The bank representatives were rather stern and stoic until I explained to them why the new tower was void of hospital patients. The tower could not get a certificate of occupancy because it was considered unsafe, given it was built slightly crooked. If you placed a patient gurney against one wall and let it go, it would roll across the floor and bang into the opposite wall.

At that point the youngest of the three bankers became animated to the point his neck veins were popping as he leaned out of his chair and over the table glaring angrily at me and remarked in unmistakably clear but not family-friendly English, "Mr. Scanlan you are telling me

Business Practices, Biblical Promises

you built a tower that is crooked? You actually put up a crooked building!" He was so enraged the most senior of the bankers asked him to sit back down and said he would take over the meeting from that point. I explained, of course, I couldn't build a thing! I told the bankers that my only role as the interim chief financial officer was to help get the organization back to appropriate operational and financial health.

The "remedy" or punishment if you will, for this company's violations of its debt agreements resulted in even more stringent financial agreements being placed on it by the banks for five ensuing years. With its business flexibility further compromised the hospital shortly thereafter ended up being sold to a larger company. Indeed, the borrower is "slave" to the lender. Debt must be used wisely because the lender is in the driver's seat of a business, just as it is in one's personal financial life. In fact, the Bible even counsels us to beware about co-signing for debts. (Proverbs 22:26, 27)

Many businesses and leaders can't imagine operating without using debt to fuel their businesses; however, there are companies who manage to do so quite well. *USA Today* did an analysis of publicly traded companies who reported having no debt for ten straight years. The stock prices of these five companies—Intuitive Surgical, F5 Networks, T. Rowe Price, Expeditors International and Paychex—went up an average of 370% over the studied time period from 2005 to 2015. Four of these five companies outperformed the stock market indices for that period. One conclusion of this research highlighted "that financial engineering by adding leverage isn't necessarily needed for solid returns."[17]

Debt is a critical performance metric which must be vigilantly monitored. Debt will impact your cash position and strategic flexibility. If deemed necessary to use, do so prayerfully and with the utmost wisdom.

God's scorecard for measuring performance

Given the data and information-centric culture for which we measure business success, what does the Bible say about measuring progress against our plan to fulfill our mission? Let's take a look:

- Before the results of our work are even known, do we think about what is *true and right* in our approach and process to work? (Philippians 4:8) Thinking ahead and thinking about a *process* which is pleasing to God is the role of the decision maker who desires to honor the Lord.
- Do we allow the results to tell the story, or do we use creative accounting and statistics to salvage the desired narrative? "I will make *justice* the measuring line, and *righteousness* the plumb line." (Isaiah 28:17) The Lord's standard does not allow for deceit, lying or stealing. (Leviticus 19:11) "The Lord detests differing weights, and dishonest scales do not please him." (Proverbs 20:23) Can we look at our key metrics and have

peace knowing they are the result of doing our work in a right and just matter?

- Are we paying a *fair wage* to those who carry out the work, (Deuteronomy 24: 14, 15) be it employees, contractors or consultants? Do we appreciate their situation and challenges, and keep close to their needs? (Proverbs 27:23) A fair minimum wage is a fiercely debated financial and political theme of our time.

- Do the outcomes and results leave enough room to handle an unexpected crisis, (Proverbs 22:3; 27:12) or to take advantage of a strategic opportunity that presents itself? A wise leader prepares for down cycles and is ready to invest when opportunities arise; however, a foolish leader lives on the edge. (Proverbs 21: 20) "As we have opportunity, let us do good to all people." (Galatians 6:10)

- Does the scorecard of our business or our personal life reflect where our *heart* is, who we are serving? God wants our heart, He knows our *motives*. Take the long view, "store up for yourselves treasures in heaven…for where your treasure is, there your heart will be also." (Matthew 6: 20,21)

- Does our scorecard reflect our *obedience and faithfulness* to God? "It is required that those who have been given a trust must prove faithful." (1 Corinthians 4:2) We are to be prepared and ready to take a stand (Jeremiah 1:17) rather than becoming ensnared into a culture of quick fixes, political correctness and godlessness. Furthermore, we are to be faithful in the position we hold today. God will not bless us if we can't be trusted with our current responsibility. "Whoever can be trusted with very little can also be trusted with much, and whoever is dishonest with very little will also be dishonest with much." (Luke 16:10) By *justice* a leader brings stability to his or her sphere of influence, but for those who are greedy, missions and plans are compromised. (Proverbs 29:4)

Let's take the scorecard upon which your performance or your company's performance is judged and view it through the screen for which God evaluates performance. Remember, God measures "success" by very different metrics then perhaps many of us tend to think and act upon. We'll use an acronym, **FOR TRUTH**, which will be easy to remember. How does your scorecard measure up against God's standard, FOR TRUTH:

Business Practices, Biblical Promises

Faithfulness to God, family and employer, in this order

Obedience to God's Word (Bible) and expectations

Right policies, numbers, dollars, statistics, measurements; truthfulness over expedience

Thought and work processes that are sound

Room to invest in opportunities

Unexpected downturns taken into account (vs. living on the edge)

Treatment of employees, customers and vendors which reflects justice and honesty

Heart motive, or are we at peace with the fact that our scorecard reflects God is first in our lives?

So, how does your scorecard and metrics measure up against the standard **FOR TRUTH?**

As Martin Luther King, Jr. once said, "The ultimate measure of a man is not where he stands in moments of comfort and convenience, but where he stands at times of challenge and controversy."[18]

The apostle Paul states, no matter what happens, "conduct yourselves in a manner worthy of the gospel of Christ" and be prepared to "stand firm." (Philippians 1: 27) "A good name is more desirable than great riches." (Proverbs 22:1) Dignity is one of God's metrics.

God indeed uses different standards to judge the inward motives and outward results of our work. The ultimate evaluation of our performance will be to someday hear the words of God: "Well done, good and faithful servant." (Matthew 25: 23) Who you are is far more important than what you do!

Chapter 8 Self-Assessment:
Metrics and Milestones: *Measuring* Our Progress

Reflections:

1. Is your company "results" or "process" oriented?
2. Are you a "results oriented" leader?
3. Are you honoring God in the way you achieve results?
4. Would you describe your company as "too big to fail?"
5. Do you know how much debt your company has incurred?

Action Steps:

1. Take the results of the key metrics, milestones and score cards used to judge *your* performance and compare those results and accomplishments against the acronym FOR TRUTH used at the end of the chapter.
2. Do the same, if you are able, with your company's key metrics—compare it to FOR TRUTH.
3. How much personal debt do you have? Draw up a specific plan to become debt free.

Key Bible Verses: Read and contemplate Deuteronomy 8: 17,18; Proverbs 23: 4,5; Acts 5: 1-11; 1 Corinthians 4:1-5; Philippians 4: 4-9, emphasis on verse 9, putting our beliefs into practice; in other words, walking the talk!

Chapter 8: Footnotes

1. Jason Gay, "The Lessons of Mariano Rivera," *The Wall Street Journal,* (March 11, 2013), p. B8.
2. Mark Puente and Zack Sampson, "Jobs chief suspended," *Tampa Bay Times,* (February 2, 2018), p.1.
3. Michael Rapoport and Dave Michaels, "SEC Keeps Heat on Non-GAAP Metrics." *The Wall Street Journal,* (May 19, 2016), p. C3.
4. Aaron Beam with Chris Warner, *HealthSouth: The Wagon to Disaster,* (Wagon Publishing, Fairhope, Alabama, 2009), pp 108,109, 132, 133.
5. Aaron Beam, "Learned the hard way," *Modern Healthcare* (February 8, 2010), p. 25.
6. Takashi Mouchizuki, "Blame Is Laid on Chiefs at Toshiba," *The Wall Street Journal,* (July 21, 2015), p. B3.
7. Matthew Goldstein, *"Judge in Dewey & LeBoeuf Fraud Case Whittles Down Charges."* New York Times, (http://www.nytimes.com/2016/02/27/business/deal/book/judge-in-dewey-leboeuf-fraud-case-whittles-down-charges.html) (accessed June 10, 2016).
8. Frank Charles Thompson, DD., Ph.D., *The New Life Chain Reference Bible,* King James Version, (B.B. Kirkbride Bible Co., Inc., Indianapolis, Indiana, 1964), p. 238.

9. Will Connors, Paulo Trevisani and Paul Kiernan, "Oil Giant Rocked by Widening Probe," *The Wall Street Journal,* (November 15-16, 2014), p. B1.

10. Aruna Viswanatha and Jeffrey T. Lewis, "Brazil's Oil Giant Pays $853 Million in Probe," *The Wall Street Journal,* (September 28, 2018), p. A1.

11. Michael Calia, "Hertz Accounting Woes Grow," *The Wall Street Journal,* (November 15-16, 2014), p. B3.

12. Joe Burns, "Audit find UMES is missing grant payment," *The Baltimore Sun,* (November 15, 2014), p. 3.

13. Justin Fenton, "Businessman charged with fraud," *The Baltimore Sun,* (November 15, 2014), p.12.

14. Rebecca Davis O'Brien, Dave Michaels and Michael Rapoport, "Former KPMG Executives Charged," *The Wall Street Journal* (January 23, 2018), p. B1.

15. Spencer Jakab, "GE's Bad New Shows Ugly Truth," *The Wall Street Journal* (January 25, 2018), p. B14.

16. Peggy Noonan, *The Time of Our Lives,* (New York: The Twelve, Hachette Book Group, Inc., 2015), p. 363.

17. Matt Krantz, "Rich investors owe thanks to these 5 debt-free companies, *USA Today,* (December 16, 2015), p. 1B.

18. Goodreads quotes, *"Martin Luther King,"* (http://www.goodreads.com/quotes/search?utf8=%E2%9C593&q=Martin+Luther+King&commit=Search) (accessed May 29, 2016).

Larry Scanlan

Part III:

When Things Go South It Means I Failed... *Or Does It?*

Larry Scanlan

Chapter 9

Testing and Trials: Stuff Happens... Or It Soon Will!

Adverse events can seemingly come out of nowhere. The Bible warns us that adversity will be part of our careers, businesses and lives. This is symbolically illustrated in the story in the New Testament in which Jesus and His management team, the disciples, got into a boat to cross to the other side of the Sea of Galilee, when, "suddenly a furious storm came up on the lake, so that the waves swept over the boat." (Matthew 8: 24) We will have more than one storm in our careers. Some storms will indeed arise unexpectedly while others, though seemingly sudden, slowly stir up when warning signs are ignored.

Adversity will come...often with criticism

On the advice of our attorney I once had to file a legal cross claim on behalf of my hospital against a physician being sued by a patient. The physician went wild and attempted to stir up the medical staff and seek my resignation as CEO of the hospital. That challenge occurred on my third day on the job. So much for a honeymoon, I was learning quickly thick skin was needed to sit in that seat.

Crises are part of our career development, as God uses business storms to prepare us for bigger and perhaps more consequential challenges later in in our careers. After all, the Bible says, "if you falter in a time of trouble, how small is your strength!" (Proverbs 24:10). It also states, "let us not become weary in doing good, for at the proper time we will reap a harvest if we do not give up." (Galatians 6:9) People of faith will have troubles and tests as they endeavor to walk with God. Crises build perseverance and perseverance leads to our character development. (Romans 5:3, 4) Yes, it is hard to keep this perspective while going through tough times; however, we can look back and probably see where good came out of most crises.

When things go south, go seriously wrong, you can rest assured that criticism and blame will be part and parcel of the crisis itself. None of us like or want adversity, criticism or undue stress in our jobs, but such is an inevitable part of life. If we are serious about our walk with God, we are told that "everyone who wants to live a godly life in Christ Jesus will be persecuted." (2 Timothy 3: 12) Note the word *everyone* in this verse. Our walk with God will, to some degree within God's providence, involve difficult and uncomfortable situations.

Look at just a few of the situations where Jesus, of all people,

Business Practices, Biblical Promises

was criticized or held under scrutiny:

- When Jesus observed people using the temple for business instead of prayer, he cleared them out. Having their market share and incomes compromised, the leaders were angry and desired to kill Him. (Luke 19: 45-48)

- Jesus saved two men from great physical pain and anguish, but in doing so, it cost the farmers some of their animals—in this case, pigs. When the people in town learned this healing cost assets, a couple of animals, they asked Him to leave their region. (Matthew 8: 28-34) It's one thing to toss a consultant out of your place of work, but Jesus?

- When He raised Lazarus from being dead, rather than celebrating the miracle the religious leaders were furious. Wanting to do anything to protect their own power base, they used this miracle as the catalyst to formally plot the death of Jesus. (John 11: 43-53)

- When Jesus was nailed to the cross and greatly suffering, not only was he criticized and mocked by his accusers standing below, the two other people crucified with him were unified in yelling insults at Him. Picture that scene for a moment— two criminals suffering on a cross somehow mustering up the strength to criticize the one man who was *not* a criminal. (Matthew 27:38, 44)   One of these mockers would soon have a change of heart.

If that is how Jesus was treated, we should be fully aware that adversity and criticism come with the territory of difference makers, especially those living out faith-based values. When there is serious crisis or controversy, criticism at times will be intense.

In the New Testament, missionaries Paul and Silas freed a slave girl who had been turned into a fortune teller making considerable money for her owners who were furious she was freed and made false accusations against the two. When there is a sum of money at stake, normally intelligent people can become irrational in their quest to keep as much of the currency pie for themselves. In the case of Paul and Silas, a mob mentality led them to being put in prison. (Acts 16: 16-24)

One afternoon I was listening to a sports radio station while driving. The commentator on ESPN was remarking how he admired the faith of an assistant basketball coach who spoke at a memorial for his own wife. She had been killed in a car accident, and three of his children were injured.[1]

The basketball coach, Monty Williams, thanked people for praying for him and his family. He then asked people to also pray for the other family involved, as the driver of that car also died in this tragic accident. He not only expressed no ill will toward that family but said his own family lived by a sign hung in their home: 'as for me and my house, we will serve the Lord."[2]   The ESPN commentator mentioned how he admired the faith of Coach Williams. He further opined his observation that people with strong faith seem to get through crises better than those absent such faith.

Well, the next several segments of the sports program were wild. In the commentators' words, he was "getting killed" via twitter and email. He read some of the feedback blasting him for bringing up faith, one saying he just alienated his entire audience. Several atheists chimed in about how they didn't need faith to get through crises, offended such a conversation had been even been brought up.

Later on this same day I opened up my daily email from the Chronicle of Higher Education. One of the featured topics was about Williams College administrators uninviting a conservative speaker because they considered his views to constitute "hate speech." This incident was the second of its kind; it followed a previous withdrawn invitation to another speaker four months prior because her views on feminism did not fall into the accepted narrative—on a college campus![3]

Mentioning "the Lord" and faith or expressing a view contrary to a particular group can be viewed as offensive and draw you into a firestorm of adversity. We should all take note, because everyone is going to have to deal with some level of adversity and criticism. Be aware, and be prepared.

Can we prepare for adversity?

Our businesses and careers will go in directions we never

planned or desired. How can we prepare when some storms come at us seemingly out of the blue while others gradually creep into our professions? We'll focus on six areas that will help us weather the storms of our professional and personal lives.

Know what you believe and why you believe it.

Early in my consulting career, our young, small company faced a serious crisis; we were down to just one job, with no other work in the pipeline. We had a memorable, pivotal meeting called by the two principal owners about whether to continue the business or shut it down.

It was also unforgettable because it was held in a convent, the sponsors of our one and only client. It was one of those days you never forget in business.

We critiqued our services, checked our references. We *believed* in the services we offered the industry and why we thought our business model fit the times. We doubled our efforts and rebounded. We kept to our business plan. I continued to work hard and prayed. We focused on doing a really good job for our clients while also aggressively prospecting for more work via personal visits, calls, emails and letters.

Little did we know that time of adversity would be the catalyst propelling us to become a respected nationally known consulting firm. Significant growth came out of that scary business crisis, as our company's revenues thereafter grew year after year.

Business Practices, Biblical Promises

The Lord counsels Christians to understand that adversity and evil prevail here on earth, affecting our businesses, government and major cultural institutions. People of faith are like sheep among wolves, so be ready, be prepared. (Matthew 10:16) The first thing to examine within one's heart, soul and intellect is specifically what you believe about God and why.

A few years ago I was in a dinner conversation with my then-teenage grandson, Airick. We discussed the ultimate question a person has to answer for themselves in life: who is your God?

If it is not God the Father as revealed to us through the Bible, then someone or something else will be our god. This could be any number of things: money, a job, sex, drugs, alcohol, position, power, material possessions, false religions, a boss, a politician, popularity, political ideology, etc.

The point is, something or someone will become central to how we think and act. We are instructed to be prepared to give an answer for what we believe (I Peter 3:15). We must answer that question for ourselves before we can adequately share and express it with other people. Knowing what we believe provides spiritual and mental peace during times of adversity and crisis.

When Jesus appeared after his resurrection to the disciples, he engaged in a conversation with Peter. He asked him three times if he, Peter, loved Him, the Lord. Remember, this same Peter had denied Jesus three times prior to His crucifixion. Peter clearly had learned his lesson and was fully prepared to make Jesus his Lord. Then Jesus indicated to him that his love of his Lord would cost him suffering while on earth.

Peter asked what would happen to another disciple, in this case he pointed to John, and said "what about him?" Jesus told him what happens to others was none of his business, but that he, Peter was responsible for his decisions, actions and reactions in this life. (John 21: 15-22) We are individually responsible for our decisions.

Jesus asked the ultimate question we all have to answer in one way or another: "Who do you say I am?" (Matthew 16:15) One can't sufficiently be prepared to face adversity and put it into proper perspective until we first answer this question for ourselves. Who is Jesus? This is the one decision in life that is permanent. Once answered, we then have a spiritual context to make a meaningful difference even in difficult times.

Prioritize and act on what you believe.

A few years ago, Hobby Lobby decided to defend its corporate values by challenging the Obamacare mandate that employers provide contraceptive coverage for their employees. The owners went through a lengthy legal process culminating in their case making it to the United States Supreme Court. In 2014 they prevailed, winning their case. Despite a costly process, the company put a priority on their values and acted upon them.

Business Practices, Biblical Promises

Is what we portend to believe really a priority in our lives? We act on what we prioritize. If we are prioritizing that which is not in our plan we either have a bad plan or inappropriate priorities.

It always amazes me how various public opinion surveys indicate that most people in our country consider themselves Christians. Our country would likely not be in the trouble it is in if we actually acted upon that which we say we believe. Our beliefs provide us a spiritual and moral compass; our actions provide outward evidence we believe it enough to actually live it.

In the story of Mary and Martha hosting Jesus in their home, Mary chose to spend time with Jesus, while Martha was distracted by the details of meal preparation. Both had the same choice to make—what to do in Jesus' presence. Martha complained about how busy she was and wanted Mary to help her. Jesus told Martha that her sister had chosen the better priority. (Luke 10: 38-41) Ouch!

Remember, Jesus never promised an easy life on this earth, but He did promise a full life, and eternal life for those who love Him. Contrast this to those who live for other gods which only serve to steal, kill, or destroy the blessings God wishes to provide upon all He has created. (John 10:10) "What good will it be for someone to gain the whole world, yet forfeit their soul? Or what can anyone give in exchange for their soul?" (Matthew 16: 26) Jesus challenges us to prioritize our faith, to not only hear His Word (James 1:19) but to actually do what it says, to "put it into practice." (Luke 6:47)

See the big picture—adversity is a refinement process to make us even better.

I hope I never forget what I once heard a wonderful minister say about life's storms and adversity. When we are truly seeking to live in a manner that honors God, He will at times test our faithfulness. When we are disobedient God will discipline us out of love because He wants us to be better people. He truly desires to bless us.

After they sinned, remember Adam and Eve tried to hide, but God pursued them. When we fail, God pursues us because he wants what is best for us. God pursues all of us; one has to consciously reject His promptings if he or she would rather serve other gods. Remember, we are *tested* for our faithfulness, *disciplined* for our disobedience. We need to keep the big picture in mind. Jesus himself set the big picture, telling us, "In this world you will have trouble. But take heart! I have overcome the world," and "I have told you these things, so that in me you may have peace." (John 16:33)

Peter describes our periods of testing as a refinement process so that our faith, being more valuable than gold, will prove to be genuine. (1 Peter 1:6, 7) A faith not tested is probably a faith not worth living.

Coach John Harbaugh of the Baltimore Ravens football team had concluded a very difficult season in 2015. He reflected that adversity made him not only a better coach, but a better person. "Some of us never realize because we don't want to look at or we don't want to deal with the things that we need to get better at. In the Bible, it talks about pruning. To me, that's really what it is—things that I didn't even know that I needed to get better at going through this season—I said 'Oh, man, I need to learn this lesson, and this is why this is happening.' You just make a decision that you're not going to fail. I don't want to fail. I don't want to be blind to it. I need to learn here."[4]   One of the jobs of a leader is to define reality; to do otherwise is to set ourselves up for even greater crises.

If we are insulted and criticized or going through difficulty for the name of Christ we will be blessed by God. Choose to praise and trust God rather than choosing misery or a 'woe is me' attitude. Our trials are a sign of God's approval of our faith, not a personal punishment. We strive to persevere and commit to continuing to do good while remaining faithful to God's work (1 Peter 4: 14, 16, 19), and learn from our season of trial and adversity.

Remember nothing can happen or touch us without God's permissive will. Our current trials and storms are refining us to make us better servants for other opportunities and blessings God is preparing us.

Watch for warning signs and take action when possible.

Even though adverse circumstances can truly come upon us suddenly, most organizational or career troubles are preceded with subtle or not so subtle warning signs. In all of my experiences with distressed organizations, only a few problems could be said to be sudden crises—the vast majority ignored indicators signaling the need for corrections or adjustments which were ignored.

I recently provided coaching to an educational institution that had declining numbers and a seriously deteriorating cash situation. The board was surprised when I pointed out the decline had been going on for five consecutive years. I have rarely seen a troubled organization for which I could not trace the source of its downfall back to the board room, where management and/or the board of directors ignored or failed to act on the need for obvious corrective action.

The same could be said of our careers or our lives; we often know by the knot in our stomach we are off track. God gave us an intellect to act upon warning signs, not to ignore them or put them in "park."

We are counseled in God's word to "be alert and self-controlled." (1 Thessalonians 5:6)[5] Jesus himself said to "keep watch" (Mark 13: 35), be aware of the spiritual context, the big picture of what is going on, and act on that upon which we are capable of taking action. Businesses often get into crisis mode when their leaders ignore those early signs, somehow thinking things will get better with time. Perhaps believing we can spare people pain, we choose to ignore those signs. The inevitable remedy is usually even more painful, and thus a sweet spot for consultants and lawyers to make a living!

Surround yourself with people who can encourage you.

I recall a time when the former television and movie star Annette Funicello was questioned by reporters in the late 1980's upon revealing she had been diagnosed with multiple sclerosis (MS). She was asked how she could go on knowing she had an incurable disease. She answered that sufferings are a part of one's life, especially one out of your control, but misery is a choice.

What a great answer. She chose not to be miserable, but rather focused on her joy and thankfulness for the many blessings she enjoyed, including a fabulous career. She chose to put life in perspective and realized that adverse circumstances are indeed part of a business, a career, a life. Being miserable however is a choice. She lived twenty-five more years before passing away in 2013.

The apostle Paul had his share of adversity and crises during his missionary career. During such times a person can feel very lonely. Paul was so lonely at one point he lost a bit of perspective when he stated, "everyone in the province of Asia has deserted me." (2 Timothy 1: 15) At times he even mentions names of people who let him down. (2 Timothy 1: 15; 4:10, 14) Probably every leader at some point in their career can identify with the feelings of betrayal and loneliness expressed by Paul.

It's important to be part of a group that can pray and support you in good times as well as in times of deep crises. Be involved in a Bible believing local church and consider associating with a smaller group of people with whom you can share your life and career paths, such as a small group Bible study. If possible seek out prayer partners at your place of work. Any number of social media venues has faith-based groups which can be a source of encouragement.

Paul acknowledged and was thankful for those who stood by

him, prayed for him and shared his passion for the mission being undertaken. (2 Timothy 1:16-18) We all need people who pray for us and with us.

Make a difference by encouraging others.

People need you to encourage them and pray for them. We have an opportunity for a greater impact in our sphere of influence as we engage with others. As we go through business and career storms we expand our experiences and skills without realizing it.

Suppose you are the leader of an organization or perhaps of a unit, department or division of a hospital. How might you feel emotionally and intellectually when you learn:

- A doctor performs arthroscopic surgery on the wrong knee of a woman. Upon realizing his mistake, he goes ahead and operates on the other knee.
- Five days later, a man has a leg amputated. When he wakes up he has to inform the doctor that he took off the wrong leg!
- Eleven days after this episode, a mistake in patient identification leads to a breathing tube being pulled from a tracheotomy hole of an elderly patient and he dies.
- If all this is not already beyond belief, days later following a birth by Cesarean section, a woman is additionally undergoing a sterilization procedure

when her doctors realize she did not request or authorize the procedure!

A hospital that had been in business for twenty-six years had its reputation shredded, ironically, in a period of twenty-six days as these incidents became a national true story. It was the brunt of late night television comedians Jay Leno and David Letterman, with the latter quipping with one line on his infamous top ten list, "you go in for routine surgery, you come out with a tail!"[6] If you were the leader of this hospital, would you expect to keep your job?

This organization experienced horrendous crises and fell under intense public scrutiny. As the local, national and regulatory spotlight became more intense people watched the CEO's actions and reactions. Through his entire tenure, he had built a high level of trust with his board, medical staff and employees and believed the organization was better than these embarrassing incidents.

He did not wallow in despair wondering why all of this happened. Having faith in God, he focused on taking action as he came to realize he was being scrutinized. He didn't try to become a different person, he stayed true to himself. For instance, his employees were used to seeing him walking the halls and engaging staff. He didn't hide; rather he continued doing so, encouraging his team and engendering confidence throughout the organization that they would get through this disaster.

He and his organization critiqued their processes and protocols and amazingly survived this calamity. They learned from it, and continue today to provide healthcare services to their community, enjoying a good reputation. Not only did the CEO come through this intense storm with God's help, but he developed a new skill set without even realizing it.

In the ensuing years he become a de facto crisis advisor, as other executives from around the entire country called upon him for advice on how to handle their own adverse events.[7] His organization's gut-wrenching and high profile trial refined him to later help and encourage numerous other leaders going through their own intense and unwelcomed catastrophes.

If you're seeking wisdom in a time of painful crisis, pour yourself into God's Word and seek the advice of men and women who have had their own share of challenging seasons in their career. As I heard someone once say, there are five gospels: Matthew, Mark, Luke and John and the fifth Gospel, *you and I*—and chances are few people will ever read the first four!

Chapter 9 Self-Assessment: Testing and Trials: Stuff Happens…Or It Soon Will!

Reflections:

1. Do you know spiritually what you believe and why?
2. Do you really live out what you believe at work?
3. Can you look back on a crisis you went through and see any good that came from it?
4. Have you surrounded yourself with a few people who pray for you? You for them?

Action Steps:

1. Write or type your spiritual testimony or conversion experience. It will help you know what you believe and why.
2. Is there a time you had warning signs but ignored them, which resulted in a significant crisis? Write down what you learned from this experience.
3. Try to name five business associates who pray for you regularly. If not name three or at least name one.
4. Write down who you pray for regularly.
5. What are the lessons learned from the greatest crises you experienced in your career? Write about it.

Key Bible Verses: Read and contemplate John 16:33 and 14:27; Romans 5:1-5; 2 Timothy 3:10-16; and James 1: 2, 3 and 12

Chapter 9 Footnotes

1. Dan Lebatard Show, ESPN radio, February 19, 2016.
2. Alysha Tsuji, "Thunder's Monty Williams shows forgiveness, compassion for driver who killed his wife." (http://ftw.usatoday.com/2016/02/oklahoma-city-thunder-month-williams-wife-ingrid-funeral-forgiveness) (accessed February 20, 2016).
3. Nick DeSantis, "Williams College President Calls Off Speech by Controversial Conservative Writer." (http://chronicle.com/blogs/ticker/williams-college-president-calls-off-speech-by-controversial-conservative-writer/108744?cid=pm&utm_source=pm&utm_me) (accessed February 23, 2016).
4. Jeff Zrebiec, "Balancing Act." *The Baltimore Sun,* (January 3, 2016, p. 3.
5. *The Life Application Bible,* (Tyndale House Publishers, Inc., Wheaton, Illinois, and Zondervan Publishing House, Grand Rapides, Michigan, 1991), p. 2175
6. Mike Clary, "String of Errors Put Florida Hospital on the Critical List." (http://articles.lastimes.com/print/1995-04-

14/news/mn-54645_1_american-hospital). (accessed February 16, 2016).

7. Norman Stein, retired CEO, University Community Hospital, Tampa, Florida, interview with author, Dade City, Florida, May 4, 2016.

Larry Scanlan

Chapter 10

Complacency and Compromise...
Twin Killers of Businesses and Careers

In making difficult business and career decisions, two seemingly easier ways to minimize the risk and consequences of standing on Godly principles is to ignore reality, or, alternatively, choose to "fit in," avoiding conflict and undue pressure. Many choose one of these alternatives.

For instance, General Electric's decline in financial performance in recent years was exacerbated by what's been termed as "success theater." The leadership of the company projected optimism about the company's performance that didn't always match the reality of its operations, markets or its declining stock price.

A culture of confidence seeped through levels of management resulting in unreachable metrics and unwise decisions. Eventually a credibility gap emerged from what was portrayed versus what was real.[1]

Complacency

In another scenario, two organizations were in discussions about a possible hospital merger. Both decided the process would be best served by engaging an outside facilitator who could objectively lead the process. The CEOs of both companies submitted names and agreed they would interview two candidates. If they agreed upon one, that consultant would be hired as the facilitator.

The CEO of the smaller hospital was a humble guy, Mr. Henry (not his real name) who earned his grey hair through the hard work of rising through the ranks. The red highlights of his face gave the impression of an Irishman who enjoyed a drink or two after work. The CEO of the larger, dominant organization (let's call him Mr. Mason) was a tall man who carried himself with a certain air of sophistication and confidence begetting a sense of importance.

I was honored to be one of the finalists interviewing with the two CEOs. The interview with Mr. Henry went well, but I knew the interview with the larger organization would likely take on a different dynamic. Mr. Mason had a recognizable name in the industry largely fostered by his self-proclaimed expertise on quality processes. When it came time to meet with him he brought along his Board Chairperson, likely a power move to impress me with his and his organization's importance to the industry.

Mr. Mason did not disappoint me, living up to my expectations. He regaled me on how his organization's quality control processes had been learned and imported from an internationally known manufacturing company which he had visited many times, and

Business Practices, Biblical Promises

further talked about how he had become familiar with their executives. In his view his organization was in a class within the industry where others would like to be.

I sat there in amazement and wondered to myself if this man had recently looked at the news links on his smart phone, or perhaps glanced at the newspaper sitting on the counter outside his office. The news headlines that very day, as well as those the previous and subsequent days, were about serious faulty design and manufacturing mistakes of this same "world-class quality" manufacturer, resulting in thousands of recalls. I could not believe he would link his organization's name to this manufacturer, at least at this point in time.

After the meeting Mr. Henry called me and asked me how the meeting went with Mr. Mason. I said, "Before I answer that, let me be sure I'm clear on something you previously mentioned to me. Is this intended to be a merger of equals?"

Mr. Henry responded, "it's the key underlying principle of the proposed transaction."

Then I suggested to him, "rather than me tell you how I think the meeting went, do me a favor and ask some specific questions at the next meeting of your joint task force" (which was shepherding the merger discussions), "and after that I will tell you how I think my interview went." He said ok and I proceeded to give him the questions to ask.

About two weeks later Mr. Henry called and told me they had their joint meeting and were able to work those questions into the discussion.

"How'd it go?" I asked.

"We called off the merger," he answered, and went on, "how did you know Mr. Mason and his organization were not interested in a merger of equals? We totally missed it and we have been in discussions with him for months."

I responded to him that anyone who was so arrogant and so fixated on his own reputation is an executive who has no equals in his mind. He certainly had significant accomplishments in his career but sometimes success breeds complacency.

Reputations can be built on accomplishments from the past and borrowed for the present. In this case, he thought he could "roll over" the smaller organization, along with a facilitator. His intent was for Mr. Henry's hospital to "sign on" for a merger in which he already knew he would never let the "little guy" have any significant say or input, let alone allow him to be his equal.

A definition of the word complacency is "self-satisfaction,"[2] a smugness or arrogance. Smugness would be the best adjective to describe the CEO described above.

Complacency is about self-comfort. Complacency is an attitude, a disease if you will, that will derail any career, business or even a country. It has been that way for thousands of years.

In a story from the Old Testament, the King of Assyria, Shennacherib, threatened to invade Jerusalem around 700 BC, telling

Business Practices, Biblical Promises

their leader that they were kidding themselves for thinking God could save them. He reminded them to look at his country's incredible past success with their string of conquests.

But complacency cost the king dearly; he lost 185,000 men and Jerusalem was spared. Later the king's own sons killed him. (II Kings chapters 18-19) The Bible warns against becoming complacent and turning our backs on God through misplaced security and comfort affecting our decision making and actions. (Isaiah 32:9-11)

The sweat and intellect required for success develops our character, which later gets revealed—sometimes when difficult circumstances arise, but more often than not during periods when everything seems okay. It's kind of ironic. We immediately know a crisis is a test, but fail to realize tests can also come in times of ease.

"When the going gets good, it can be tough to avoid overconfidence."[3] This quote was made by Justin Lahart of *The Wall Street Journal* in reference to United Continental Airline's decision to expand available seat miles pursuant in part to better than expected fourth quarter earnings. The reporter observed, "It is easy to tell a story in which more people take to the skies as global standards of living rise and corporate budgets expand. Companies can tell themselves those kinds of stories when times are good. After so many years of feast, though, airlines risk forgetting all about famine."[4]

Complacency can blind our ability to plan for an inevitable downturn in the economy or the rise of a disruptive competitor. Remember, before implementing strategic actions, review the past, "the ancient ways" for lessons learned.

To become successful requires preparation, hard work, focus and perseverance. But once some level of success is achieved one soon realizes to sustain that success takes even more work and becomes a daily challenge. Testing during times of trial or comfort will bring out our true character.

When I became a Chief Financial Officer (CFO) I felt good that in our first month we performed well and hit our important targets; but as a young executive, one big adjustment was coming to the realization that there was no rest. I had to leave the finance committee meeting and be immediately about the business of achieving this same success the next month, and then the next month, and so on.

One does not achieve on-going success absent excellent work habits, discipline, and accountability. This is difficult for many people; it becomes easy, almost natural, to relax and let your guard down when business seems to be going well.

After the Old Testament leader Nehemiah led his people to rebuild the wall of Jerusalem in the amazing short stint of just fifty-two days, he went back to Babylon for a period of time. Upon returning to Jerusalem he astonishingly observed his people had become self-satisfied, with protocols and processes being sloppily handled or ignored. Nehemiah's absence along with an insufficient accountability system fostered a complacent culture. (Nehemiah Chapter 13) Complacency is an attitude that justifies short cuts in

Business Practices, Biblical Promises

both protocols and execution eventually resulting in a business and career being adversely affected.

In the early months of my first role as a financial officer I went to the CEO and said I was looking for documentation on how our healthcare organization set hospital room rates but had not found any. The CEO said we didn't have any such documents, so I asked him how our hospital set room rates? He responded that we simply waited for the competitor fifteen miles down the road to announce their rate increase and we followed whatever they did.

Given our need for more capital dollars to fund strategic and routine maintenance projects, I said we couldn't wait that long. I then proposed preparing an analysis of our funding needs to support immediate room rate increases. A few days after providing the CEO with my analysis he called me into his office. He said he agreed with the workplan and with my recommendation for an immediate price increase, but he could not present this to the Board of Directors. I was surprised, so I asked him why not. He responded, "Because I would get fired. But, I would like you to come and present your recommendation, they might believe you." (translation: they might not and thus fire me).

I tripped onto a hot spot of sensitivity for the board of directors because room rate increases always brought press coverage, which was always unwelcomed by the board. Furthermore, the local business community especially resented such increases, and would make future Chamber of Commerce and service organization meetings uncomfortable for a while.

Larry Scanlan

Usually the only management person who came to board meetings in this organization was the CEO. So here I was, a new CFO, going to my first board meeting and making a presentation on a topic the board really did not want to hear, let alone handle.

I made the presentation (long before the days of power point, I might add) with my heart beating faster than normal, yet confident that my rationale and recommendation would be best for the organization's on-going financial viability. After I was finished, I sat down and the board chair, a rather dictatorial character, asked the board members if there was any interest in making a motion on "Mr. Scanlan's proposal?"

One member raised his hand and said he felt my presentation was outstanding with clear rationale and went and on and on for about a minute about how wonderful it was and then made the motion. Then another board member raised his hand and said, "I must say, I did not understand a single (bleeping) word Mr. Scanlan said, but it sounded so good I will second the motion!" God in his wisdom and humor sometimes has a way of humbling us before we even have the chance to allow ourselves to get puffed up. Our recommendation to increase room rates passed. My boss was happy he kept his job, and I survived my first board meeting and could make my mortgage payment that month!

In setting room rates according to those set by the competing hospital down the road, our organization had lost its discipline to manage effectively toward what was in the best interests of our business and our customers. We had taken the easy way out and had become complacent. Our competitor was the leading hospital in the entire region. They were doing what was best for them, which was one reason why they were the leader. We had become followers, doing just okay as an organization, quite comfortable with mediocrity.

I call this the "blue angel" method of management. Those world class jet pilots known as the "Blue Angels" majestically fly in formation and perform all kinds of maneuvers in various formations, up, down, sideways, you name it. It's beautiful to watch. But what happens if you are flying behind the lead jet, solely focused on it and not sufficiently tuned in to the reality of your own surroundings, and the lead jet hits a mountain? You're going into the mountain along with the pilot ahead of you.

Complacency will compromise purpose and discipline, leading any business or career into trouble. It's like this in our spiritual life also. When we let our guard down and become distracted by someone or something (such as small "g" gods) rather than pleasing God, we set ourselves up for setback and failure. Awareness of our actual spiritual state, personal priorities and business environment are good inoculators against complacency.

Compromise

The sister of complacency is compromise. One definition of compromise is "a concession to something derogatory or prejudicial."[5] Compromising on clear Biblical principles usually leads to making *un*wise decisions. So it behooves a leader to be in God's word in order to understand Biblical guidelines.

The Bible gives guidance for our collective good. There are numerous areas in business and life which present appropriate opportunities to compromise and reach mutual agreements without negating faith-based beliefs. Wise leaders recognize the clarity or freedom of Biblical guidance and therefore know when compromise is appropriate and when it is not.

In another real-life scenario, after having just made a speech at a regional healthcare conference attended by several hundred upper and mid-level executives, I exited the stage and sat down in the audience to listen to one of the speakers who followed me, in this case the CEO of a national association. He was speaking on the subject of business ethics. A number of times during his talk he referenced and touted a specific healthcare company that had once violated legal and ethical guidelines for which the government had fined and placed them under a government consent order. The speaker's point was that this company had learned its lesson on the merits of ethical reporting and compliance and now was *the* model for ethics and accountability for other companies to follow.

I sat and listened with a great deal of skepticism because I knew something about this company. They were capable of doing many things right, but I also knew their true ethical compass pointed green, meaning they primarily cared about the bottom line and meeting investors' expectations. I figured they would live within the rules when quarterly targets and expectations were met, but their instinctive mode of operation would be to bend them when things weren't going their way.

The speaker's praise about the company's ethical reporting and compliance all went out the window less than a year later. The government charged the company for violating the very same behaviors for which they had previously been convicted. Absent a financial moral compass, compromise was in the DNA of this company!

Compromise of faith-based principles can be defined as "half-way" leadership— it takes away from our full effectiveness of having a Godly influence on our organization and customers. In the Old Testament Jehu became King of Israel around 841 BC. He did many things right, particularly in destroying the evil influence from the previous dynasty of King Ahab. He eliminated Baal worship, a form of idolatry; however he allowed the worship of golden calves which violated God's commandments. In other words, he was not "all in." Jehu provided lip service in regard to worshipping idols by exercising political correctness when it came to certain popular cultural practices. Despite some good things he accomplished, his tenure was considered mediocre. (II Kings 10:30, 31)

No matter if you agree or disagree with a leader's vision or politics I think almost everyone is uneasy with half-way leadership. It serves no good useful lasting purpose, and ultimately adversely impacts those under such leadership.

Reading and studying the Bible will help us to *know the essentials* of our faith, which should not be compromised. "The word of God is alive and active…it judges the thoughts and attitudes of the heart" (Hebrews 4:12).

The non-essentials of one's faith are also areas of opportunity for compromise. Christians can agree or disagree on areas of business policy and practices that are not contrary to God's Word. My company may be more environmentally friendly than your company, but the fundamentals of our faith are not compromised by our views on this issue. We may agree or disagree on a proposal to tax one business more than another business. For instance, business travelers pay substantial taxes on things like hotel and rental car taxes, something non-travelers don't face. These are non-essential areas of one's faith. Taxes can be compromised through legislation or regulation, they can be changed without compromising one's basic tenets of faith. If I don't belong to a union but I am mandated to pay union dues I have legal options to explore which won't comprise my faith.

But the fundamental tenets of God's Word, the essentials, must be adhered to no matter what. For instance, if a company's (or government's) medical benefits mandate that all employees pay for "reproductive prevention" services then the essentials of our faith are in play, given the potential interference with God-created life. The Lord summarized all of the commandments in just two: love God and love other people with all your mind, heart, soul and body. (Mark

Business Practices, Biblical Promises

12: 30, 31) If a man or woman is blessed with great intellect and skills but lacks genuine reverence for God and concern for people, then we really have nothing of lasting significance. (1 Corinthians 13: 1-3)

A fundamental right, the freedom of religion, was one of the cornerstones of our country's founding. It now is challenged widely throughout our culture, legislatures, executive branches and courts to a point where our society is becoming free *from* religion, absent of faith-based values. One writer referred to this as the "Pharaoh Effect" in reference to the Old Testament story of Joseph. Joseph was essentially the chief operating officer (Prime Minister) of Egypt, saving his people from a great famine. Some years later after Joseph and his generation passed away and a new leader took over, a dim view was taken of Joseph and his team's achievements. In fact, the new King wasn't even aware of Joseph or his accomplishments. Bent on enforcing conformity with social policy, a crackdown on the people took place and Jews were forced into slavery,[6] hard work, and even into killing of all male babies. (Exodus 1)

Pressures to conform to social policy are impacting business and religious institutions in today's society. For instance, after years of the U.S. Conference on Catholic Bishops and the federal government cooperating in fighting human trafficking, the Obama administration nullified the Catholic contract because it did not offer abortion, contraception and sterilization services.[7] Businesses have been forced to bring lawsuits to protect their right to decline to underwrite such services. The pressure to conform and compromise to politically correct social policy is significant. All faith-based believers will be increasingly faced with dilemmas that will test their faith, love and concern for people. They may even have to put their careers, job tenures, and financial security on the line.

In the book of Revelation, the church of Pergamum, a sophisticated Greek city, was surrounded by Satan worship. Believers were under tremendous pressure to compromise or forsake their faith, yet most remained true under very difficult cultural and religious pressures. One member is even mentioned by name, Antipas, because he refused to compromise and was put to death for the steadfastness to his faith. (Revelation 2: 12, 13)

Another body of believers, the church in Thyatira, a secular blue-collar city with no particular religious focus, did a lot of good works but also allowed compromise to creep in by tolerating a belief promoted by some that sexual immorality was not a serious sin for believers. (Revelations 2:18-22)

In Pilate's administration of Jesus' trial, he compromised his way out of a difficult set of circumstances because he feared the implications for his own leadership tenure and administration. He literally washed his hands of the decision to crucify Jesus by telling the gathered crowd "I am innocent of this man's blood, it is your responsibility." (Matthew 27:24)

And in more recent times, who can forget the brutal beheadings

Business Practices, Biblical Promises

by ISIS in February 2017 of twenty-one Coptic Christians for refusing to deny their faith in Christ. There was no compromising by those courageous martyrs, all beheaded for their refusal to denounce their faith or accept conversion to another religion which would have preserved their lives.

One evening I heard an interview on cable television with Aaron and Melissa Klein, the couple who lost their bakery business for not making a wedding cake for a same-sex couple in 2013, a case that garnered wide spread publicity. The steep fine of $135,000 imposed on their small business by the State of Oregon in 2015 forced them to shut it down. In December of 2017, they lost their appeal with the Oregon Court of Appeals.

The interviewer asked the couple how they felt about their decision in light of all that had transpired over the years since they lost their business. The young man answered candidly saying he could not have imagined the magnitude of the fallout they would experience over the years as a result of their decision, but they would still make that same decision again. As he courageously articulated, Christ is first and they as a couple "were all in" no matter the cost, and for them that cost has been great.

Many people, including Christians, would differ on the rationale used by this couple. You may or may not agree with their business decision, but for them there would be no compromise for their deeply held faith.

Warning signs of complacency and compromise

I have had my share of experiences winning clients because they missed the warning signs of complacency or compromise, and as a result, needed our consulting assistance.

I had one health system client who experienced high labor costs, paying wages much higher than its surrounding competitors. Eventually the management team realized they finally had to deal with their labor cost challenge. Rather than be branded with having layoffs on their watch they merged with another organization. In their minds the merger would be the "cover" for cutting costs.

In this case complacency led to a compromised strategy as the organization merged and dealt with the labor cost issue through the cover of "merger efficiencies."

God's Word provides "yellow" warning signs for each of us to avoid the lethargy of complacency or the quagmire of compromise. Here are some warning signs for each of us to heed:

- When we have less of a desire to read and study God's word, or worse, we are hardly reading it in the first place. (Romans 10:17) "Woe to you who are complacent." (Amos 6:1)
- Giving little or no thought to God in our lives, forgetting about Him. (Psalm 106: 7, 13)
- Giving into our own selfish desires and cravings. (Psalm 106: 14)
- Despising God, not really believing in Him, in essence provoking the Lord. (Psalm 106:24, 29)

- Worshipping someone else or something else. (Psalm 106:36) In the book of Zephaniah the Lord warns those practicing false worship that He will "punish those who are complacent." (Zephaniah 1:12)
- Entering into inappropriate alliances or compromising cultures. (Psalm 106: 35; 2 Corinthians 6: 14-18)
- Serving two masters, trying to live Godly but also fitting neatly into a godless culture. (Psalm 119:113)

King David actually prayed for God to replace complacent and compromising leaders (Psalm 109:8) with other men and women willing to step into those demanding roles. Though complacency or compromise might appear for a while to benefit our businesses or ourselves, leaders "cannot be established through wickedness and the righteous cannot be uprooted." (Proverbs 12:3) Godly leaders should choose to take a stand and make a difference, regardless of the slanted views of the media.

One Old Testament leader probably few have heard of is a man named Phinehas (Aaron's grandson). He is described as one who was zealous for the honor of his God. He took a stand against godless practices and it ended up saving a nation from self-destruction by making atonement for the country's compromising behavior with pagan religions and cultures. Before Phinehas's intervention God had planned on punishing all those who had compromised their faith, but because of Phinehas, He spared them. (Numbers 25: 6-13; Psalm 106:30) We need such leaders today in our businesses, educational, government and cultural institutions.

Given the diminishing influence of Judeo-Christian tenets in our society it is probable the ensuring months and years will bring pressures on all of us to compromise on God's Word and our faith. Our beliefs will be put to the test. Through our seasons of trials we are to demonstrate our love and concern for others, be they friend or enemy. (I John 2:3-11)

One such test is taking place in western Canada. In 2005, Canada legalized same-sex marriage, promising traditional religious values would continue to be honored. In 2012, Trinity Western University in British Columbia, a Christian school, decided to open a law school. Several provincial law societies protested the application, calling the students and faculty bigots and worse because of their adherence to their beliefs that same-sex marriage was un-Godly.

After several years of legal proceedings in June 2018, the Court ruled against opening the law school because "accrediting a school that upholds traditional Christian teachings on marriage could send the wrong message to Canadians who disagree with Trinity's beliefs." The President of the University responded "we are disappointed but we are not deterred. Despite the blow, Trinity will stand firm in its beliefs." He went on to remark about how the university's students positively impact various parts of the world through their ministry work, and how they plan to continue to spread their love and skills.[8]

I once brought a stack of business books to a department meeting in a hospital. I wanted to visually challenge the group to read various business stories to stretch their minds and imagine what we could accomplish as a team. One of the books in that stack was my Bible.

After the meeting I learned that one manager was very upset I had the nerve to bring a Bible to a business meeting in a secular hospital. She was a person who was influential in the community and was formerly a member of the board of directors of this organization.

The point I tried to make to her was the Bible is full of commandments and principles applicable to building a successful business. I survived her criticism and tried my best to demonstrate love and concern in our business relationship, but I know she was one happy woman a few years later when I left to work for another company.

None of us knows how we will react when our faith is tested; however, our awareness of the warning signs of complacency and compromise below will provide a sound foundation for our subsequent decisions:

- Inconsistency in our daily time of deliberate prayer and Bible study
- Thinking more about ourselves and our agenda rather than the Lord's

- Contemplating decisions that are clearly against God's Word
- Being involved with inappropriate alliances and/or cultures
- Placing God second to small "g" gods dominating our life

Jesus himself summed it up; He expects our total dedication. He does not want the Christian's life to plateau with the comfort of complacency or be tarnished through unwise compromise. He wants us to be "all-in"— "No one who puts his hand to the plow and looks back is fit for the service in the kingdom of God." (Luke 9:62)

Chapter 10 Self-Assessment:
Compromise and Complacency: Twin Killers of Businesses and Careers

Reflections:

1. Have you ever worked in a company you would say was complacent?
2. Have you ever experienced a time of complacency in your career?
3. Does your company compromise to achieve needed results?
4. Did you go along with the company narrative in such cases?
5. Will you take a different stand in the future?

Action Steps:

This is a very personal exercise: honestly evaluate where you are currently on the warning signs of complacency and compromise—It could save your career! (Rate the following):

<u>Never/Sometimes/Almost Always</u>

I read-study the Bible almost daily:
I think of God often during the day:
My decisions and actions are
   mainly about me:

                                                            Never/Sometimes/Almost Always

I separate faith from my work:

Other "gods" are more important:

I'm involved in inappropriate
   alliances/relationships:

I try to fit into the culture and not
   "rock the boat":

Key Bible Verses: Read and contemplate: Isaiah 32: 9-14; Psalm 119:113; read Psalm 106 in its entirety; 2 Corinthians 6:14-18 regarding alliances; and Luke 9: 57-62 on being "all-in" for Christ.

Chapter 10: Footnotes

1. Thomas Gryta, Joann S. Lublin and David Benoit, " 'Success Theater' Masked Rot at GE," *The Wall Street Journal,* (February 22, 2018), pp. A1,2.
2. Merriam-Webster's *Collegiate Dictionary, Eleventh Edition* (Merriam-Webster, Inc., Springfield, Massachusetts, 2014), p. 253.
3. Justin Lahart, "United Risks Sparking A Price War," *The Wall Street Journal* (January 25, 2018), p. B14
4. Ibid.

5. Merriam-Webster's *Collegiate Dictionary, Eleventh Edition* (Merriam-Webster, Inc., Springfield, Massachusetts, 2014), p. 256.
6. Kevin Seamus Hasson, "Watch Out for the Pharaoh Effect," *The Wall Street Journal,* (August 29, 2014), p. A 11.
7. Ibid.
8. Bob Kuhn, "Canada Attacks Religious Freedom," *The Wall Street Journal* (June 22, 2018), p.A13.

Larry Scanlan

Chapter 11

Profiles in Perseverance

Things will indeed go south during the course of one's professional career. For those who attempt to live a Biblically-based faith, that faith will bring both opportunity and stress. Testing and trials are indeed part of life. Misery, complacency, compromise, and quitting don't have to be—they are choices. Perseverance is also a choice.

In 2008, my wife and I were in London. Her birthday occurred during this trip and as a gift I was able to secure two VIP tickets to see comedian Joan Rivers.

Upon arriving that evening at the dimly lit theater the venue for the show was a bit startling. I don't think there were more than a dozen rows of seats; perhaps the auditorium fit 125 people or so. It was a very small theater with a proportionally small stage. Joan Rivers put on a show that was about her life. She had a few talented professionals' who would play her as she might look in her younger years, but a good portion of the show was a one-lady act; it was Joan and it was about Joan. As good as the acting and laughter were that evening it was the power of her life story that captivated the audience.

Professionally, after reaching international star status, Joan Rivers told how she got her own TV show, but how it was slotted in those days against the one and only late-night talk show king, comedian Johnny Carson. Ironically, he had given Joan her big break in show business. Carson was furious upon learning of Joan taking a competing time slot. Joan called him to try to explain her reasoning but he hung up and never spoke to her again despite her attempts on several occasions to reach out to him. She said she still grieved that Johnny went to his grave without her being able to reconcile their relationship; you could sense her pain remained.

Moreover, Carson was powerful, and entertainment executives knew his value and power, so Joan ended up getting blackballed from American entertainment. Her career plummeted. If that were not enough, her personal life was shattered when her husband committed suicide. That caused a tremendous strain with her daughter as the guilt and blame for the suicide ripped the mother-daughter relationship apart. It would take years to heal.

Joan talked about the loneliness of those years, and the misperceptions of fame. She recounted a story about the "famous" movie actor Mae West, who Joan revered. When Mae West died, Joan felt compelled to go to her funeral; she was astonished to find she was the only person that showed up. So much for fame.

Joan Rivers concluded her show standing front- and- center of the small stage with her arms fully stretched out to each side and said to us, "this is my life now; I play in theaters like this where tonight maybe we have seventy-five people in the audience."

Her show was well done, her story a mixture of comedy and tragedy, both funny and humbling. Most professionals will never experience her magnitude of adversity in their careers and personal lives. No one would have blamed her if she packed it in and quit. But for whatever reason she felt her calling was to entertain, so she humbled herself to play whenever and wherever she was given an opportunity.

She had been in the limelight for years and was going through a season of life where her fame was barely flickering, her visibility no longer part of the American entertainment scene. But quitting was not for Joan Rivers. She persevered believing her talent was to be used to entertain people.

Not long after we met Joan, her life took a wonderful turn to be followed by a stunning ending. She made an amazing professional comeback and was once again a standout on American television, hosting a popular fashion show and partnering with her reconciled daughter on a reality show. One season she even won the competition on Donald Trump's "Celebrity Apprentice" television series.

She could not have known if she ever again would become a star, but she never gave up and she made her way back. Whether or not you cared for her form of entertainment is not the point. This was a person who persevered as a professional until her very last breath; therein is the tragic ending following her unlikely comeback.

Joan underwent what we would call a routine medical procedure in 2014, an upper endoscopy at a New York City ambulatory surgery center. It's a procedure I have had at least twenty-five times. The professional staff, perhaps sidetracked a bit by the personality asleep before them, became complacent in their processes. They compromised their protocols and professional discipline and in one instance, reportedly took pictures of their unconscious patient. Probably having done these procedures hundreds of times they likely thought no one would find out. Somehow things went south—Joan never woke up and died a week later.

A tragic irony. Here, one person who experienced significant professional setbacks along with heart-breaking personal tragedy had chosen to persevere through all of this. Meanwhile, a small group of medical people with a chance to serve this patient made a decision to become complacent with the opportunity before them.

I suspect it was not the first time such complacency occurred. Short-cuts eventually become habits. It's quite a study in contrasts—perseverance versus complacency and compromise—and a lesson for each of us to take away and contemplate. Joan left this earth successfully honoring her calling as a comedian to the very end, while the medical professionals, facing a malpractice filing for their choice of complacency and unprofessionalism, settled the case in 2016.[1]

Business Practices, Biblical Promises

Perspective: Key to persevering

God calls Christians to a higher purpose: to live with an eternal perspective, not just for the things of this earth which will be left behind. (Matthew 6:19-21) The apostle Paul counsels and encourages us to "never tire of doing what is right." (2 Thessalonians 3:13) [2] This seems like a very high bar. It's one which Joan Rivers achieved no matter if her audience numbered in the thousands, hundreds, or merely dozens.

I sometimes try to picture what it would have been like to be Noah or someone in his family when he was building the Ark. It had never rained from the sky, and here Noah was building a boat. He worked on this project faithfully for over one-hundred years. Imagine the ridicule he must have received. His world was like our world, with plenty of self-centered people doing what felt good to them and all kinds of evil imbedded in the culture of that time.

But Noah did not go along with the crowd. He persevered, he kept plugging away even though nothing in his work provided visible evidence to give him the satisfaction or adrenalin lift most of us need to keep going. Imagine yourself in that kind of circumstance.

Most of us need some feedback loop to know we are on the right track. How did he keep going? Why? He had a quiet heartfelt belief his purpose had meaning. His faith in God was not constrained or measured by the circumstances or culture in which he found. Imagine what people thought and said about Noah. No matter, he never tired of doing what was right.

Furthermore, Noah wasn't engaging in a selfish act. God in fact stretched out Noah's work for over a century to give people the chance to change their ways before His judgment was commenced through the Great Flood. Though it made no logical or common sense until that day the rains came, Noah worked some 120 years after commencing his profession as a shipbuilder. Talk about perseverance!

Perseverance: opportunity to make a defining difference

God has provided difference makers through the ages who are of great encouragement to us when facing difficult circumstances. One author researched successful business, sports and military leaders to determine the essential qualities of their success. He found two. The first he described as a combination of tenacity, courage, seriousness, steadfastness—in other words, perseverance. The other was ironclad emotional control.

He cited George Washington as an example of a difference maker that possessed both qualities. "In the end, the source of Washington's greatness was simple, even if it wasn't easy to pull off. It was a function of the choices he made consistently, every day, in darkness or light."[3]

A modest-sized business known as Conestoga Wood Company was founded in 1964 and is headquartered in the little town of East Earl, Pennsylvania, just outside of Lancaster. For a few years I lived just a few miles from this company. They serve the kitchen and bath industry, making cabinets and wood products.

The 2010 Affordable Care Act regulations mandated for-profit businesses to provide contraceptives. The owners knew this requirement violated their Christian beliefs. They filed a lawsuit while complying with the mandate because the fines for not doing so would have cost their business $38 million a year. Working its way through the courts with appeals, eventually the United State Supreme Court combined Hobby Lobby's similar case with Conestoga Wood. In June of 2014 the Supreme Court ruled in their favor. As Conestoga Wood's CEO Anthony Hahn said, "This effort wasn't just for Conestoga. We took this stand for others as well." [4]

We as individual professionals have the opportunity during our own periods of challenge and struggle to make a profound difference in the world. A young lady volunteered to join an aid organization whose mission encompassed helping the people of Afghanistan rebuild their lives after the Taliban had been driven out following the aftermath of Sept. 11th, 2001.

While working with a social services organization she faced significant pressure to be converted to becoming a Muslim. This provided the opportunity to tell her friends that she "followed the Honorable Jesus Messiah." But she needed to be very discerning about such conversations, constantly aware of the social rules and local customs that need to be followed which were important to her own safety.

Larry Scanlan

Women had a certain place, and what one said, how it was said and even whether you looked someone in the eye could jeopardize one's life. She became aware of physical threats, including kidnapping. (Some medical and social workers did lose their lives in their volunteer work in that country).

When given the opportunity she shared her faith with great compassion through simple stories from the Bible as her new friends would attentively listen. Her love and service to the Afghans allowed her to answer their questions, some out of curiosity as to why she, an American, would travel so far, and travel alone at that, to serve their war-torn country. Though her work was appreciated by those she and her team served, her faith was a threat to some of the power brokers, enforcers and religious leaders.

After serving and persevering for five years, she and her team had to leave quickly as illegal gangs and local militias grew in strength to the point where the number of kidnappings and killings were growing. Walking down the street, or riding in a rickshaw, or drinking tea in a neighbor's home all became too dangerous. She left with a duffel bag, backpack and stories from a group of people she grew to deeply love.

Perseverance isn't about marking time, it's about faithfulness to that which God has called you and for which you have sufficiently prepared for service. She persevered through this season of her life, came back to the United States and wrote a book about her experience, *In The Land Of Blue Burqas."* She wrote it under the pseudonym, Kate McCord, primarily for the protection of those she worked with and served in Afghanistan.[5] She didn't have a fancy title, she was an aid worker in her organization, but what a difference she made to those she served.

Other medical and social aid workers, missionaries, and Christians living out their lives and purpose are not so fortunate, as they are being martyred for their faith and their work. Most Christian martyrs up until this point have not been Americans, as non-westerners have borne most of the risk of suffering the ultimate fate for their faith.[6]

At the turn of the 20th century the Middle East was comprised of about a twenty percent Christian population, but today that number is less than ten percent and dwindling. Intolerant governments and radical groups are driving them away, kidnapping, or killing people of Christian and Jewish faiths. For many of those who survive, their faith has cost them their homes, businesses and whatever few liberties they may have enjoyed.

The non-profit group Open Doors documents that Islamic extremism is the lead cause of persecution for seventy percent of the top fifty countries on its watch list. The most dangerous country is communist North Korea.[7] Christians living in oppressed countries need our prayers.

They are mentors of perseverance because Christians in the United States will face increasing pressure to suppress Christian values from the public and professional arena. Most of you are aware of the pressures and legal threats facing Christians who seek to publicly pray on school grounds or pray in Jesus' name at other public events such as high school football games, graduation ceremonies and civic events. Looking at current events and trends, I believe the effort to remove Judeo-Christian values from the public marketplace is and will continue to be relentless.

When the words "Merry Christmas" are considered controversial you can bet this is just the beginning. A couple of years ago I said "Merry Christmas" to the cashier at a convenience store, a top of the mind regional chain, as I was completing payment for my purchase. The young lady looked at me in bewilderment. I think she wanted to reciprocate but was fearful of doing so. So she turned to her supervisor and asked if it was ok to say "Merry Christmas" back to me. I was within hearing distance and listened as the supervisor counseled the employee that it was ok to respond since I brought up those two words first, but she as an employee was never to initiate such a greeting!

I followed-up this business encounter by writing a letter and later having a telephone conversation with the company's vice-president of human resources. He assured me thereafter that retail clerks were free to initiate "Merry Christmas" greetings if they were comfortable doing so. I continue to monitor if this is indeed the case.

This story of verbalizing Merry Christmas may seem like a very small if not silly example of "persecution," just an inconvenience for

Business Practices, Biblical Promises

Christians justified by the need to be more sensitive to those offended by Christmas. But, keep in mind the ability to silence seemingly small areas of faith-based values will make it easier to later stamp out more consequential religious practices. Remember, in your decision making, opposition, especially in areas of essential Biblical principles, often means its time to take a stand!

A time and a season for perseverance

Perseverance doesn't always mean staying in the same occupation forever. The young lady serving in Afghanistan fulfilled what she set out to do during the five long years she remained; each day she had opportunities to serve but they also carried with them daily threats to her very being. In God's mysterious ways, there is a time for everything and a season for every activity, a time to serve and a time to move on; (Ecclesiastes 3: 1, 6) however, within each of our seasons of life God calls us to sustain our love and our efforts, to persevere.

Sometimes we have the God given wisdom to know that it's time to change or move on. Other times life events will cause a different direction in our lives. Some of these changes we will not welcome, like losing our jobs or our businesses or our health, or suffering other painful losses and experiences.

Marie is the president of her own consulting firm which she started in 2008. In the mid 1990's she was in charge of a division of a business, but mired in an organization with a boss who did not respect her opinion nor want her advice. Her job became highly frustrating. She eventually left the organization, an end to that season of her professional life.

Their loss was our gain, as her employer had been our client and we saw her talents first-hand; she was truly a gifted professional. We hired her and she was a highly valued contributor to our company for a number of years. About a year after we sold our company to a publicly traded firm she felt it was time for another season of life and she moved on.

Up until this point, Marie had persevered through corporate jobs in various seasons of life, never seriously giving any thought to establishing her own business. But once she left our company she finally did and has been highly successful running her own firm for the last ten years. To put it in her words, "I never imagined I would be doing anything like this-and didn't even know there was a 'this.' Most importantly, I always believed that the only place I ever wanted to be was in the center of God's will for my life-and that there was a purpose and a plan even if I didn't always see it or understand it. Nothing in life was worth anything without that. I'm still curious about what's next as I transition out of work to more free time as I near retirement. I still feel like there's something worthwhile that lies ahead but I have no ideas what it is."[8] Though a successful entrepreneur of her own company Marie is already anticipating that her retirement years will present another season of service.

God decides when the seasons of life change. In His providence He may lead us to a different venue (employer) or a different role, or a new geography where our staying power and "stick-to-it-ness" is then carried into another area of service for another season of life. At times we might lose our perspective through times of turmoil, but nothing touches the Christian absent God's permissive will. While we might lose awareness of Him in our periods of fear or loneliness, He will never lose sight of us. (Matthew 14: 27; Luke 12: 4-7)

    The New Testament missionary, Paul, was effective because he persevered. Unlike some TV preachers of our day who dress in expensive suits seemingly matching a materialistic lifestyle, Paul was out with the people. His teachings were not the prosperity gospel—he taught *the* Gospel, which some did not want to hear; the reception of his preaching was no different back then than it is today. He asked what each of us needs to ask ourselves, "Am I now trying to win the approval of human beings, or of God? Or am I trying to please people? If I were still trying to please people, I would not be a servant of Christ." (Galatians 1:10)

    Paul's seasons of life, like ours, was comprised of good times and bad times. "I have learned to be content whatever the circumstances. I know what it is to be in need, and I know what it is to have plenty." (Philippians 4: 11, 12) At times, he would find himself in prison. During such low seasons of his life he persevered, even bringing the Gospel news to fellow prisoners and guards.

    Another time Paul, along with his "business partner," Barnabas, were preaching when a group opposed to them came along and turned the crowd against them. They stoned Paul and dragged him out of the town, leaving him on the ground because they were sure he was dead. But, with the help of his friends he got up and kept on going. Why? Paul said it best: "we are not only to believe in Jesus, but also be willing to suffer for Him," (Philippians 1: 29), to persevere.

Toward the end of Paul's life he was placed under house arrest in Rome. His final season of perseverance would allow him a unique opportunity to bring the gospel to the leaders and politicians who held the center of power during his lifetime, the Roman Empire. Paul, the man who once jailed and killed Christians, died in service for His Lord bringing the gospel to the most politically powerful people of his time.

For a short season of my life I attended a church in Lancaster, Pennsylvania. There was a family there that had a son who was a missionary, Chet Bitterman, who our local church helped and supported.

He and his wife joined Wycliffe Bible Translators to bring the Bible into local tribal villages. The place where he and his wife and others were living in Bogota, Columbia was invaded in January 1981. They were looking to kidnap the leader of the mission, but he was not there at that moment, so they took Chet. They wanted the work these missionaries were doing to stop, and to drive them out of the country.

After forty-eight days being held hostage, Chet Bitterman was found dead on the side of a road. Applications to serve with Wycliffe doubled in the year following Chet's martyrdom as others looked to step up and answer the cause for Christ.[9] We never know the breadth and depth our perseverance will have on others.

But where is God in our times of adversity?

The Old Testament Book of Job describes the life and trials of a wealthy professional named Job who lost everything—his family, his job, his assets, his health, and his reputation. What else was there to lose? Through these trials, he tried to keep his faith focused, "The Lord gave and the Lord has taken away, may the name of the Lord be praised." (Job 1:21b) How many of us could keep such a perspective?

But other times he questioned God at length and tried to figure out why all of this happened, bewildered about his dire circumstances. We all likely have asked God the same questions at various points in our lives.

However, God did not directly answer Job. Rather God asked Job questions, a lot of questions, covering four chapters. (Job 38 to 41) The questions asked of Job help him realize God is so big and yet so very detailed we cannot comprehend such Holiness, "how great is God—beyond our understanding." (Job 36: 26)

God's character is not on trial through our adverse seasons of life, it is rather our own character! Three responses are available to us:

    1) we can reject God,

    2) we can try to explain away adversity or blame it away, or,

3) we can trust God in both the dark seasons of life as well as the bright ones.

Some professional and personal difficulties lack rational human explanation, such as was the case with Job. He questioned God, but did not reject Him. He could not explain why these tragedies happened to him and those he loved, nor did he accept the counsel of his "friends" who said he himself was to blame.

When things go south it does not mean it is necessarily our fault or of our own doing. After examining his own heart and motives, Job made a decision to trust God's promises even though nothing in his life made sense. Job's perseverance and faithfulness were rewarded with the latter part of his life being more blessed than the first part of his life. (Job 42:12)

Job's circumstances resulted in highly unusual and intense trials. God chose to reward him while he had life left to live on this earth. God may choose to reward some who persevere with blessings on earth, while for others those blessings will occur in Heaven, where such blessings are not temporal, but eternal. In fact, Jesus said that when we are persecuted because of Him, our reward in heaven will be great. (Matthew 5: 11, 12)

A high ranking naval officer gave a commencement address and used the thirty-six years of his Navy SEAL experience to encourage, inspire and challenge the new graduates as they looked forward to their futures. He told stories of his training and experiences as a SEAL, just as our own career experiences train us for future missions and careers.

In one training exercise, the SEALS practice underwater attacks on enemy ships. This practice entails swimming underwater for two miles at night using nothing but a depth gauge and compass to focus on what lies ahead. In approaching the target ship the light begins to fade the deeper you go into the water as the ship itself blocks any moonlight that might be overhead. You have to find the centerline of the ship, the deepest and darkest part of the ship where you can't even see your own hands in front of your face. The noise from the ship is so deafening you can become disoriented.

The Admiral said, "Every SEAL knows that under the keel, at the darkest moment of the mission, is the time when you must be calm, composed—when all your tactical skills, your physical power and all of your inner strength must be brought to bear." He then concludes with this key takeaway for those who want to make a difference: "If you want to change the world, you must be your very best in the darkest moment."[10]

Chapter 11 Self-Assessment:
Profiles in Perseverance

Reflections:

1. Are you going through a difficult time of testing and trial now?
2. Do you believe God is on trial during such circumstances?
3. Do you find yourself reading the Bible and praying more during such times?
4. Do you believe in your difficult times God has lessons for you to learn?
5. Do you believe God can eventually use your situation to help others?

Action Steps:

1. Think of a particularly painful time of trouble and trials you had in your professional career. Write about how you got through it. Answer the following:
    a. What were one or two key takeaways from your experience?
    b. Were you eventually able to grow from this and help others?
    c. Can you now look back and see God's hand in the situation?

2. If you are in a good season of your business and career consider one or two ways you can use your current blessings to help encourage or mentor another professional man or woman, especially those going through difficult challenges.
3. Whatever season you are in, thank God for what He will do or has already done—He will always be with you! Take a few minutes and thank Him now!

Key Bible Verses: Read and contemplate Luke 12:7; Matthew 5: 11, 12; 28:20; Job chapters 38-42; Philippians 1: 29 and 4: 11, 12.

Chapter 11: Footnotes

1. Chris Spargo, "Melissa Rivers reveals tragic details behind Joan Rivers death while explaining her decision to file medical malpractice lawsuit," (http://www.dailymail.co.uk/news/article-3067244/lt-100-percent-preventable-Mellissa-Rivers-reveals-tragic-details-Joan-Rivers-death-explaining-decision-fil.) (accessed March 2, 2016).
2. *The New Life Application Bible* (Tyndale House Publishers, Inc., Wheaton, Illinois and Zondervan Publishing House, Grand Rapids, Micigan, 1991), p. 2183.
3. Sam Walker, "How to Lead Like George Washington," *The Wall Street Journal,* (September 22-23, 2018), p. B5.

4. Jeff Hawkes, "Conestoga Wood Specialties wins in Supreme Court religious freedom appeal," (http://lancasteronline.com/news/local/conestoga-wood-specialties-wins-in-supreme-court-religious-freedom-appeal/article_ac0e803e-f231-11e3-ad87-001a4bcf6878.html) (accessed March 2, 2018).
5. Kate McCord (pseudonym), *In The Land Of Blue Burqas."* (Chicago, Moody Publishers, 2012), p. 306
6. Stan Guthrie, "Martyrs in the Time of the Charity Selfie" *The Wall Street Journal* (August 22, 2014), p. A-11.
7. DeMoss, "Fact Sheet: 2017 Open Doors World Watch List," (http://www.demoss.com/newsrooms/opendoors/background/fact-sheet-2017-open-doors-world-watc-list) (accessed April 29, 2018).
8. Interview with MarieAnn Thornburg, February 1, 2018, Miami and Tampa, Florida.
9. Melissa Paredes, "A Cause Worth Living For," (http://www.wycliffe.org/blog/featured/a-cause-worth-living-for) (accessed April 29, 2018).
10. William H. McRaven, "Life Lessons From Navy SEAL Training." *The Wall Street Journal* (May 24-24, 2014), p. A11.

Chapter 12

Legacies and Epitaphs: Finishing Strong!

I went to visit a CEO of an organization located in a neighboring county for the purposes of getting to know him and assessing if there might be a way for our organizations to work together. The CEO was cordial and after our meeting he gave me a tour of his facility. At some point, we finally reached the top floor.

As we stood at this apogee, he proudly looked out the window as if he were scanning his kingdom, pointed down and said, "that will be my legacy." I looked but only saw a large parcel of land with some scattered clumps of grass so I asked exactly to what was he was referring?

He pointed again and said the area below would be transformed into a parking lot and that would be his legacy! He realized, he explained, most CEOs want a building or an invention as a legacy, but his organization did not have the capital dollars for such. He desired a legacy which his administration would someday leave to a successor; his would be a much-needed parking lot.

Larry Scanlan

Legends in our own time?

I think all of us, especially those who are leaders, want to leave a legacy no matter how big or small, something for which they get recognition and credit. Many leaders probably think the more prominent the legacy, the better. Think about many of our politicians—the higher the office held, the more they desire to leave a very visible legacy,—and (heaven forbid) if they get re-elected to an office, it seems subsequent terms become more and more wrapped up with leaving an even larger legacy. I don't know about you, but I yearn for the political leader who will focus on serving his or her constituents instead of spending so much time on a self-defined legacy.

But politicians are not the only professionals with such desires. Most of us want to leave a legacy for future leaders and followers, the intended beneficiaries of our achievements.

If you doubt one's inherited desire to leave a legacy, just look at Jesus's disciples. At the last supper Jesus told them He himself would suffer and one of the twelve would betray Him. They questioned among themselves who that may be.

But if that were not enough, the gospel account of Luke tells us a dispute broke out among them as to which of them would be considered the greatest. Imagine that scene (Luke 22:14-27)…and it wasn't the first time such a debate took place. (Luke 9:46-48) Jesus was about to commence His darkest time on earth and those closest to Him were worried about their legacies! If it can consume them, it can consume us.

Our consulting firm provided services to an organization facing operational and financial challenges. The CEO was not exactly thrilled he needed us, but he hired us.

He assigned our team some work space in a small conference room that sat directly across from the security guard. Part of his job was to be sure we consultants did not leave the conference room to roam the halls to observe operations, or worse, actually talk to people. (We found a way to do both despite the guard).

Furthermore, the security guard had two other jobs. He was to guard the life-size portrait of the CEO which hung on a wall directly behind his dais, and he had the responsibility of protecting the main door to the executive suite. His activation of a button allowed authorized visitors into the "c-suite."

All of this took place while we worked inside a building which had the last name of the CEO on the outside top corner of the building. Yes, you no longer have to be dead to leave a legacy. We were dealing with an executive who clearly was a legend in his own mind!

A number of people who have been blessed financially have given substantial donations in exchange for naming rights to such things as libraries, hospitals, educational facilities, arenas, stadiums, etc. But legacies are somewhat self-made and can be fleeting. Look at the recent movement by students at our universities seeking to remove names from buildings or remove statues. Through the eyes of a younger generation, legacy achievements and honors have been brought into question.

Princeton University has been under pressure to remove all things named in honor of former President Woodrow Wilson. Although he was considered a liberal, today students abhor that he advanced segregation.

Harvard Law School was poised to remove the name of Isaac Royall, the 18th century founder (whose bequest funded the law school), because he owned slaves.[1]

The University of Maryland removed the name Byrd (Harry C. Byrd, an All-American athlete and former President of the University) from its football stadium for similar reasons, a name that had stood for ninety years.[2]

Yes, the legacy we work so hard to create today may be viewed very differently in twenty, fifty, or a hundred years from now. Legacies are not necessarily permanent.

Legacies vs. Epitaphs

Dictionary.com defines *legacy* as something that comes from the past or something handed down from the past. Most of us have good intentions in wanting to leave an organization in better shape, we want others to know we gave it our best and, if possible, we like a little credit and appreciation for it. A legacy is something we very much have a hand in, we make the decisions and take actions that contribute to what ultimately becomes our legacy, what we leave

Business Practices, Biblical Promises

behind.

An epitaph on the other hand is a final judgment on a person rendered by a third party, again as stated in Dictionary.com We don't define it, others define it for us! Most of us have probably seen humorous commemorations or epitaphs placed as inscriptions on tombstones or monuments, such as these:[3]

Ascribed to a business professional:

"I made some good deals and I made some bad ones. I really went in the hole with this one."

Rendered to a famous TV personality who passed away about ten years ago:

"I will not be right back after this message."

Finally, a couple of epitaphs bequeathed to social media lovers:

"DIED: From not forwarding that text message to 10 people."

"Please deactivate my Facebook."

The final or ultimate assessment of our work is God, the ultimate judge. He sees through the motives behind our decisions and looks at the results of our efforts, and then pronounces the final inscription on our service. Let's look at a few epitaphs from the Bible:

- Caleb was one of the two strategic planners who brought back a positive report on assessing the merits of the Promised Land, a position contrary to the majority of those sent on the mission (Joshua was the only other member.). Caleb was forty years old when he was on that mission, in the prime of his life. He remained faithful to God and at age eighty-five received his reward of more land, "because he followed the Lord, the God of Israel, wholeheartedly." (Joshua 14: 14) Can this be said of us?

- Abimelech was a son of the great Gideon of the Old Testament. Upon Gideon's death, Abimelech saw a great opportunity to seize the leadership vacuum. He was thirsty for power and blessed with a "smooth" tongue, making him a real politician! His thirst for power was his legacy, so much so that he killed his seventy brothers to eliminate any possible competition. The allure of promotion and power can be so strong that a person loses his or her sense of fairness, sensitivity and appropriate responsibility. Most of us probably know or have worked with people who would do anything to get to the top. Abimelech made it to the top but his thirst for power caused his own tragic and ironic death. A woman dropped a millstone from the top of a tower packed with people as Abimelech attempted to set it on fire so he could kill them. The millstone cracked his skull and arrogant to the death, he asked a soldier to finish him off with a sword so it would not be said "a woman killed him." Upon his death, his epitaph read, "Thus God repaid the wickedness that Abimelech had done." (Judges 9: 51-56)

Business Practices, Biblical Promises

- Ruth's unconditional love of her mother-in-law, Naomi, was such that she willingly left her own homeland to go with Naomi to her country. A relationship of love and respect can overcome deep cultural, racial, religious and political divides, such as were prevalent in her time. Perhaps Ruth's epitaph is best described by Boaz, a very successful businessman who eventually fell in love with and married her: "all the people of my town know that you are a woman of noble character." (Ruth 3:11) How we interact with others, especially those of differing religious, racial, cultural, sexual and political preferences will, in part, define our epitaph.

- Eunice and Lois were mother and grandmother to a racially mixed, shy young man named Timothy, who became a first-generation Christian. Timothy later went on to become a missionary, partnering with Paul. Paul's tribute to Timothy's upbringing is captured in these few but powerful words: "I am reminded of your sincere faith, which first lived in your grandmother Lois and in your mother Eunice and, I am persuaded, now lives in you also." (2 Timothy 1:5) There are many fractured families where children and young people are being raised by a single parent, or by a grandparent or two, or perhaps an aunt or uncle. Can your own "sincere faith" positively influence one or more people in the remaining time you have on this earth? "Sincere faith" would be a wonderful epitaph!

Our calling and our desired legacies should be viewed through an eternal lens because the only epitaph of permanence will be inscribed by God!

When the disciples were positioning for greatness in the story referenced earlier, Jesus counseled that our status (aka epitaph) is not about being served or "getting." Rather it is about giving and serving: "for it is the one who is least among you all who is the greatest." (Luke 9:48b)

This concept of "the least being greatest" was imbedded into my business experience in a rather unique manner. Early in my consulting career our company won a substantial job to put a business plan together for two organizations that had merged. What we learned after starting the job was both stunning and humbling.

The three finalist firms submitted references of previous clients along with the contact information of the key executives, a normal request. The CEO directed his vice president of human resources to check the references submitted by the three firms. He called those references but did *not* call the listed executives. Instead, he decided to call their secretaries and administrative assistants. He simply asked them if they recognized the name of the firm and, if so, how they (the secretaries and administrative assistants) were treated.

Fortunately for our company we always went out of our way to treat such people professionally and with gratitude because they were

Business Practices, Biblical Promises

the people who moved things along and got things done (such as scheduling interviews, gathering documents and data, et cetera). In fact, at the conclusion of a job we often left behind a thank you gift for such professionals.

We learned we won this project primarily based on the experiences of "the least of these." That lesson served us well over the following decades of consulting.

Finishing our mission faithfully

No matter how successful we have been or how far short we have fallen in our professional and personal lives, finishing strong should be our goal, but it too is a high bar. It's not easy.

Several decades ago there was an educator known as the "rainmaker," because he kept significant donations coming in the door to keep the business going. By all outside observances he was successful. He enjoyed a high profile in Southern Maryland, and it seemed like almost everyone knew him or knew of him. But he tired of the pressures of leadership with its demanding schedules and constant need to raise more money all while attempting to balance out demands on the home front. So one day in the spring of 1982 he seemingly vanished—he staged his own disappearance!

He could not think of finishing, he wanted relief, so he created his own "exit strategy." He drove his car to the airport, caught a plane and never returned home, nor went back to his job as a college president. His disappearance was a mystery to his family, who didn't know if he was alive or dead…for a few years! This story eventually became the subject of a book titled, *"Exit the Rainmaker."*[4]

While on a consulting engagement in El Paso, Texas I had the opportunity to meet the former college president, Jay Carsey, and hear his story first hand some ten years after his unique disappearance. The pressures of leadership were such that he just wanted out, so he exited his business life—thus the title of the book.

I pray I can finish strong, but humanly speaking I can give no such guarantees, as the story of our college president depicts. None of us has any guarantee of finishing strong. It has been said that of the one hundred or so characters whose lives are fairly well detailed in the Bible, only one-third finished well; the rest failed in the second half or latter part of their lives.

In today's increasingly strong economy, successful business people likely have more money than ever before, which provides them with even more ways to get distracted from what is truly important.[5]

The decisions we make will go a long way in defining our true legacies and the corresponding epitaph God will render upon our work. Each choice and each action leads to and builds toward the strength of our finish.

If we are taking shortcuts now, we'll likely do so in the next phase of life. If we are self-centered or mean-spirited now, it's likely we'll be that same way the next week, next year, and in the next decade, probably only getting worse as we get older—unless we are aware of our shortcomings, decide to change and take concrete actions to do so. Nothing changes if nothing changes. Awareness and action are two necessary ingredients. Following God's Word is the other.

Some people are takers, others are givers. It's a choice. Our decisions and priorities today set the stage on how we'll finish. The apostle Paul counsels us to live life by being a blessing to others (2 Timothy 4: 6), and to conduct ourselves in a manner honoring God. (Philippians 1:27) Persevering through the various seasons of life helps refine our character. This will contribute to our being in a position to finish strong by doing what is right in God's eyes, not by the world's scorecard.

Solomon's legacy was probably being the wisest person that ever lived on this earth prior to Jesus. Solomon had leaders from other countries that would stop by to pick his brain and admire his accomplishments, and there were many. As the third king of Israel, he built the Temple and the Royal Palace. He accumulated greater wealth and wisdom than all of the other kings of his era. He had fourteen hundred chariots and twelve thousand horses. He was a builder, a trader, a diplomat, and an admirer and collector of the arts. His wisdom was astonishing, clearly God-given; but with wisdom comes great responsibility.

Solomon chose to make an ill-advised alliance with Egypt, a self-centered business decision which would prove fateful. He also made personal decisions regarding his sensual desires that compromised his work and leadership. He had seven hundred wives and three hundred concubines. His wives distracted him from what was important. Even worse, he put his own people into forced labor to build his structures. He ended up worshipping other gods, the small "g" kind of gods any of us today could be worshipping. (I Kings 10:23-11:6)

In other words, Solomon became sidetracked by people, money and things that distracted him from putting God first. What might be diverting us?

Yes, Solomon had buildings, riches and a kingdom (think business) to show as his legacy, but God had a different view, an epitaph if you will; God told Solomon "Since this is your attitude and you have not kept my covenant and my decrees which I commanded you, I will most certainly tear the kingdom away from you." (1 Kings 11: 11)

As an act of mercy and respect to Solomon's father, King David, God allowed the kingdom (company) to stand during Solomon's lifetime, but upon his death the kingdom indeed was divided. Solomon's legacy may have looked good during his lifetime, but his epitaph was a judgment on his self-centered decisions. Despite being gifted with great wisdom, he did not use it responsibly to God's honor and glory through much of his life.

Solomon was a leader like many we see today. As wise as he was, he was not content, so he tried just about everything a man could do to satisfy his own spiritual, physical and emotional desires. He had the title, power, money and fame to try just about everything and anything, and he did. After all, who could stop him?

After testing many venues to satisfy his own curiosity over a long length of time, late in his life Solomon wrote the Old Testament book of Ecclesiastes. He opened his letter summarizing a life spent seeking his own pleasures and goals: "Meaningless, meaningless, utterly meaningless! Everything is meaningless." (Ecclesiastes 1: 2,3) Wow, he began his letter as if writing his own epitaph! And it's pretty depressing. This is quite different than the legacy he desired or the one that was visible to other people.

As Solomon reflected back over his life, he was able to put it into perspective. The end of his book closes in stark contrast to the beginning, "Here is the conclusion of the matter: Fear God and keep his commandments, for this is the duty of all mankind. For God will bring every deed into judgment including every hidden thing, whether it is good or evil." (Ecclesiastes 12: 13, 14) Contemplate this counsel as it applies to your decision-making process.

Let's go from perhaps one of the smartest men in the world, Solomon, to one of the strongest men, Samson. He would have made a great television wrestling star, he was the Hulk Hogan of his era, and he too could put on a good show! If Samson had television in his era you could picture him flexing his muscles and posing that dark, well-toned body, looking into the camera and saying "What'cha gonna do when Samson-mania runs wild on y-o-u!" (Those of you who were TV wrestling fans in the eighties and nineties will get that—it's ok to admit it). In addition to his strength, Samson was also talented and did plenty of good work in his professional career. But remember he had significant blind spots in his professional and personal life, namely, his need for revenge and his weakness for illicit sensuality.

We sometimes justify good leaders who compromise their personal lives. We like to believe their professional strengths outweigh their personal weaknesses, but is this really the case? Samson went from the top of his professional life as the Judge of Israel to the bottom—landing in prison. Talk about a free fall from power. Any number of contemporary business and political leaders have had similar experiences. Though he led Israel for twenty years, Samson's life perhaps became best known for "what might have been" because his blind spots became the hallmark of a significant portion of his tenure.

But at the very end of his life, Samson realized he was off track spiritually and understood it cost him dearly in both his professional and personal life. His last act and very last breaths were spent accomplishing something with God's help that allowed Samson to finish strong.

The Philistines were celebrating their capture and punishment of Samson (they gouged out his eyes) by offering sacrifices in gratitude to their false god, Dagon. Samson was brought out from his cell to "entertain" the partying crowd of three thousand people. The crowd mocked Samson as it praised its god Dagon for the conquest over God's former leader of Israel.

While leaning back and forth between two central pillars supporting the temple, Samson asked God to give him his strength back one more time so that he could finish his life by taking out those who were worshipping false gods and torturing him. God honored his request. Samson, standing between the two pillars and strenuously pushing them outward, caused the building to collapse. He indeed died that day but also took out more enemies in that one move than he ever did when he was alive. (Judges 16: 21-30)

No matter how far we might fall, God is there to lift up a humble and contrite heart. He forgives those who genuinely seek His forgiveness. Samson's legacy might have been defined by people as "what might have been," but God's epitaph on his life placed Samson in a chapter of the Bible commonly called the "Hall of Faith" as one of those "who through faith conquered kingdoms and administered justice." (Hebrews 11: 32, 33)

We indeed serve a merciful God. If you're on a self-centered track with your life, as Samson was, today is the day to change direction. Why today? Because we don't know *when* the finish line will appear!

I worked once with a man named Leo, a chief executive officer. He was a naturally shy man and also known by many as "a religious man." There were people on his board of directors who mistook Leo's shyness as arrogance, and worse, they did not care for his type of "religion," he being a Christian of Mennonite persuasion. In this community, being prejudiced toward Mennonites would be akin to living in Rome and not caring for Catholics.

Leo's contract came up for renewal and he knew he had some enemies on the board. His organization was not in any trouble, but this was a personality clash, so he himself was in trouble. I was working the night of a board meeting and before I left to go home I walked into the administrative suite to drop off some workpapers. As I walked quietly past the CEO's office, Leo was sitting at his desk. I don't believe he ever saw me. I simply dropped off papers outside his office, glanced in, turned around and left.

But what I saw was impressive to me as a young professional. Leo clearly had been left out of or dismissed from the Board of Directors meeting. He sat at his desk devoid of any papers, with only his Bible in front of him. He was reading his Bible and praying about the outcome of the meeting and his future as the organization's chief executive. It was a humbling scene, forever seared in my mind. The outcome was not good, as later that evening a few directors came down to his office and told him he was done.

What was in fact more instructive and impacted the people who worked closely with him was how Leo persevered through this season of life. He left quietly with dignity and class. His legacy and tenure (the finish line) was in part determined by the board of directors; but, his epitaph was his faith in his Lord that he would move on to another season of life, and that his God would provide him with his next professional challenge.

The Lord did just that, providing him the opportunity to move back to the Midwest to a geographic area he and his wife dearly loved from a previous work experience as a healthcare executive in Kansas. Other people may try to define us, but only God understands our hearts when it comes to the reasoning behind our decisions and actions. He will bless and honor those who choose to honor Him, so we can finish strong!

The end is better than the beginning

The apostle Paul is perhaps a good model for most of us on how to finish strong. He was educated and had two jobs (missionary and tent maker), but had more than his share of failures and disappointments. Subsequent to becoming a Christian he learned that serving God came with its own costs. He was beaten, thrown in prison, and had his plans thwarted on more than one occasion. His career had its ups, but it also had its significant downs, including living with a painful physical challenge which Paul described as "a thorn in my flesh" which tormented him. (2 Corinthians 12: 7-9) Yet Paul wrote over half of the New Testament in the end, not to mention converted thousands, or maybe even tens of thousands of Jews and Gentiles across the world to Christianity.

No matter what our past disappointments are, each day is a gift of life and an opportunity to finish well with both the opportunities and challenges the Lord may bring. An Old Testament verse says it well: "The end of a matter is better than its beginning." (Ecclesiastes 7:8) No one finishes with a perfect record, not even close, as we all have made mistakes along with purposefully selfish decisions; (Romans 3:23) however, we don't have to stay on the self-centered track. How we finish matters.

Paul counsels and mentors us to be reading the Bible in a consistent manner, and to keep using the God given gifts He has bestowed upon each of us. He tells us to discipline our lives so that they match the doctrine we say we believe—in other words, we need to "walk the talk." This walk is hard, it requires our perseverance. (1 Timothy 4: 13-16) We are to keep our head in all situations, endure hardship, and discharge our responsibilities faithfully. (2 Timothy 4:5)

As Paul realized his own tenure was coming to an end (he would be executed in Rome under Emperor Nero), he wrote from prison, "I have fought the good fight, I have finished the race, I have kept the faith." (2 Timothy 4:7) He finished this thought by saying that he, along with all who believe, will have their epitaph and eternal reward administered by the "righteous Judge" when our time comes. (2 Timothy 4:8)

Circumstances change in business, sometimes slowly but other times with incredible speed. One day your company is doing great, and suddenly a "disruptive" entrepreneur or a behemoth competitor has turned your business seemingly upside down. Changes in technology have us running to keep up with the flow of information, let alone trying to get an edge. Sometimes government regulations or changes in political power cause disruptions of businesses and alter daily routines.

Sometimes illness causes change. A friend of mine from youth worked in education. He earned a doctorate degree and became nationally known in Christian education circles. He was hired as a principal for a school in Pennsylvania. A year into his tenure he was unexpectedly diagnosed with cancer. Not long thereafter he passed

Business Practices, Biblical Promises

away.

One might think serving a school for only a year would leave little room for a legacy. But his inspiration to his staff in allowing them to expand and stretch their skills later led to a handful of them starting their own Christian school, focusing on inner city youth. My friend was hired to be principal of one school but his legacy in death inspired a second school. God's epitaph will undoubtedly recognize his even broader impact, both that which is seen and that which we cannot see.

Difficult circumstances will undoubtedly come our way, sometimes for short periods of time (though it may not feel that way), and other difficulties might truly be long term, as in years upon years.

Jesus prepared thirty years for His ministry—for a tenure that lasted a mere three years. But His perseverance and finish left an impact that is felt to this very day. It will be felt tomorrow and the next day no matter what activist group or government body tries to restrict the impact of Jesus' ministry. And, get this, He asked us to be His representatives in this mission until His return!

How we use our God-given talents in thought, speech and action is our opportunity to leave a legacy leading to a meaningful epitaph. Preparation, priorities and perseverance are up to us. We may try to shape our legacy, but its ultimate outcome, our epitaph, is in the hands of a just, merciful and loving God. Each of us must determine who or what is central to our profession, business, and life.

Larry Scanlan

God created us, but He never forces us to serve Him; that is *the* ultimate decision we must make in life. We can't work our way into His favor, as He is holy. So, He sent his Son Jesus as His gift: "For God so loved the world that he gave his one and only Son, so that whosoever believes in him shall not perish but have eternal life." (John 3:16) His is a gift universally available to all of us but must be individually accepted or rejected—there is no in-between.

About sixty-years ago, a missionary's legacy among faith-based people was to bring the gospel to a tribe of Indians in South America, which cost him his life—he was martyred for sharing the gospel. His name was Jim Elliot. Something he penned in his journal eight years *before* his death has been used by God as his epitaph to challenge and encourage decision makers for the ages: "He is no fool who gives what he cannot keep.... to gain that which he cannot lose."[6] Or, in the words of the Gospel writer: "The world and its desires pass away, but whoever does the will of God lives forever." (1 John 2:17)

If God were to write an epitaph on your life or my life right now, what might it say? What occurred before is in the past. This season of life is your opportunity to make a difference that matters. Decide today, live it today…and tomorrow.

Remember, how you finish is what matters most. Just because things went south, it doesn't mean you are a failure. Today is a new day, a great opportunity for you to do something that will honor God. And then tomorrow, and the next day, and so on. God has good plans for you. (Jeremiah 29: 11) The apostle Peter reminds us that everything in the past will be destroyed or disappear, so look forward, not back, and choose to live holy until the day God calls you home or He returns (2 Peter 3:11-13). Live for the Lord, only He is forever. Don't worry about your legacy, leave it to God—His epitaph is all that counts!

Chapter 12 Self-Assessment: Legacies and Epitaphs: Finishing Strong!

Reflections:

1. Have you met people who seem to think they are legends in their own minds?
2. Have you consciously worked to build your own legacy?
3. Have you considered your epitaph might be quite different than your legacy?
4. Is how you finish your career and life important to you?
5. Following Christ has a cost—is He worth following in all areas of your life?

Action-Steps:

1. We all have regrets. Perhaps you've made serious mistakes that continue to weigh on you. Pray and ask God to help you put it all behind. Remember the "end of a matter is better than its beginning." (Ecclesiastes 7:8) If possible, apologize to those you have offended, ask for forgiveness and seek to reconcile.

2. In this chapter, we discussed what the apostle Paul said about finishing strong. How do you and I measure up? (1 Timothy 4: 7, 8; 2 Timothy 2: 3-7 and 4:6-8) Rate the following:

Mostly/Sometimes/Never

I read and study the Bible:

I use my talent(s) and gift(s) to help
  others and honor God:

I live a disciplined life style, I endure:

I walk the talk, I strive to be faithful
  to God:

Key Bible Verses: Read and contemplate the scripture verses cited in action steps number 1 and 2 above. Pray and take action specifically on what you will do to make the end of your work tenure and life more meaningful than the beginning. (Ecclesiastes 7:8)

Chapter 12: Footnotes

1. Christopher Caldwell, "Donor Beware," *The Wall Street Journal* (March 12-13, 2016), p. C1,2.
2. T. Rees Shapiro, "U-Md. Board of regents votes to strip Byrd name from football stadium," (https://www.washintonpost.com/news/grade-point/wp/2015/12/11/u-md-board-of-regents-votes-to-rename-brd-stad (accessed May 29, 2016).

3. 25 Of the Funniest, Weirdest & Most Unique Epitaphs You'll Ever See, (http://www.welikeviral.com/25-funniest-weirdest-unique-epitaps-youll-ever-see.htlm) (accessed May 15, 2016).
4. Jonathan Coleman, *Exit the Rainmaker,* (New York: Macmillan Publishing Company, 1989).
5. Howard Dayton, *Business God's Way,* (Orlando, Florida: Compass, 2013), p. 152
6. Billy Graham Center, (https://www2.wheaton.edu/bgc/archives/laq/20.htm.) (accessed March 15, 2016).

ACKNOWLEDGMENTS

When I heard a speaker articulate how most Bible stories of Jesus' ministry found Him engaging in the market place, it confirmed my own reading of the Bible. Indeed, through the ages people have spent a significant portion of their time in the business world. The challenge for those who love the Lord is how to make a difference beyond the pressures of the day. I began working on this book project about four years ago but its true genesis is based on my experiences, observations and reading from a career now approaching half-a-century. My interactions with people and their organizations over this span of time influenced the writing of this book.

First, I thank my wife. She is the first line of critique when I finish writing a chapter. Her career experiences of being an executive secretary to CEOs, senior management and boards of directors in industry, education and healthcare provided me with valuable "in-house" expertise! Furthermore, it is easier to concentrate on writing knowing I have the love and support of my wife and our blended family of four adult children and six-grandchildren, as well as that of my siblings, nieces and nephews.

Larry Scanlan

I must especially recognize the contribution of my late administrative assistant, Becky Rust, who passed away in 2017. Her help with the various drafts of this work was, as usual, invaluable. She was the epitome of a professional. I never met anyone like her. She was a tireless, selfless perfectionist for which I was the undeserved beneficiary. Thank you, Becky, for all you did for me over a period of twenty-five years. You were a true professional in every sense of that word.

Trusted advisors speak truth out of a heart absent their own agenda. They recognize blind spots and appreciate one's strengths. To that end, I thank several friends and wonderful professionals who took time to critique various drafts or portions of the book: Lisa Hine, Kathy Kronenberg, Dr. Bruce Main, MarieAnn North, Sara O'Brien, Fred Wickis, Jeanette Windle, and step-daughter Tricia Finck, all provided valuable feedback.

I thank those named and unnamed in this book whose stories contributed to this work— you know who you are. I have learned so much from others during my career. I truly appreciate the experiences, interaction and observations that led me to put these in writing in hopes of encouraging other business professionals to live with a Godly eternal perspective. I especially thank the principal founders of The Hunter Group (THG), David Hunter and Merrilee Gerew, for bringing me into their confidence in the running of their company. My decision to join and stay with THG proved to be the most pivotal and consequential business decision I made in the last twenty-eight years.

Finally, a big shout-out to Michele Chynoweth; without her assistance and encouragement, this book would have never seen the light of day. Michele's background as an author, book coach, educator, journalist, and businesswoman was invaluable in assisting me to keep this work "Biblical" but practical for business men and women reading it. Michele's experience in business made her a particularly relevant critic and editor for me. Additionally she filled the void and challenge I faced after my assistant Becky Rust went home to be with the Lord. Michele taught me much about writing. It's no wonder she is an award-winning author and speaker. Her honors are earned and well-deserved. Thank you, Michele.

I thank you for choosing to read this book. I hope it will encourage you to make decisions that go beyond the pressures of the moment and think about the legacy and epitaph you impart on your family, business, church and community. God blesses a heart that desires to put him first. May God abundantly bless you!

Larry Scanlan

www.ingramcontent.com/pod-product-compliance
Lightning Source LLC
Chambersburg PA
CBHW031611210526
45464CB00004B/1522